My True Reflection

freedom from eating disorders

Leigh-Ann Brisbin

Bridge-Logos

Alachua, Florida 32615

Bridge-Logos
Alachua, FL 32615USA

My True Reflection
by Leigh-Ann Brisbin

Printed in the United States of America.

Library of Congress Catalog Card Number: 2009920667
International Standard Book Number 978-0-88270-588-0

Scripture quotations in this book are from the *Holy Bible, New International Version®*. NIV®. Copyright © 1973, 1978, 1984 by International Bible Society. Used by permission of Zondervan. All rights reserved.

G218.316.N.m901.35230

Contents

A Letter of Thanks

I want to thank God first and foremost for giving me the courage to share the details of my life so that He may be glorified. I want to deeply thank my wonderful and amazing husband, Todd, for unconditionally loving me, supporting me, believing in me, never leaving my side, and encouraging me through the most difficult time of my life. You are such a gift and blessing to me. You are an example of God and truly my hero. Thank you so much for your contribution to this book and for sharing your heart as well. I know it has not been easy. Thank you for walking through this process with me, helping me to step out in faith and follow God's lead. Thank you for prayerfully helping me to make the difficult decisions.

I want to thank my children for seeing the good in me, loving me in spite of the bad and being patient when mommy CAN'T…! To my sweet Emily, thank you for your wonderfully thoughtful cards, kind words, and prayerful heart. I am so very thankful for all of your questions. Our deep conversations always remind me to remain in Him and to have a faithful heart. To my crazy Christopher, thank you for always keeping a smile on my face and a laugh in my heart; you bring me so much joy. To my darling Annaleigh, my little face of God's faithfulness, I will never forget what the Lord has brought us through together.

To my family and extended family, thank you for loving me through the hurt and fear I must have caused you. I am so sorry. Mom, you are a wonderful woman of God, and I am so thankful for your influence in my life. I am so glad that you are more than my mom but one of my very best friends. Dad, thank you so much for your love and support. Grandma, thank you for your influence, not only in my life, but in the lives of your children, grandchildren, and great grandchildren. You are the most godly woman I have ever known, walking in faith, trusting in Him, and shining his light for all to see. I am so privileged to have you in my life and to glean from your wisdom. God is still using you in such mighty ways. I love you so very much. Susan, thanks for having the vision for this book as I first began to write and encouraging me to continue pursuing publication.

I, in no way, could ever express in words, my thanks and gratitude toward my dear friend Susie. God has given me such a gift in your friendship. Your loving sacrifice, investment in my life, willingness to be on your knees in prayer for me, and continued encouragement to direct me back to the eyes of Christ far surpassed what I ever imagined someone could do for another. Your love is such a pure example of Christ's, and your life such an example of wisdom and strength as you faithfully follow your Lord and lead others to know Him more deeply.

I want to also thank my dear friends Mine, Katy, and Kristen, who stayed steadfast when I was pulling away from them and faithfully continued to pray on my behalf. A special note to Marilyn—I am still in awe of how the Lord so perfectly knitted our hearts together. You are an amazing woman and follower of God. I am honored to call you my friend. Thank you so much for your continued encouragement, influence, and prayer support in my life and through this crazy publishing process.

To the wonderful women of Riverwood, you are such a wonderful church family. Thank you for your honest hearts, your steadfast prayers, and your overwhelming support and friendship. Sarah, you are special to me in so many ways, and your friendship is priceless. Your life is an encouragement to me.

Thank you to John and Kay for your love, concern, accountability, encouragement, and friendship as I battled this so many years ago. Your influence and impact on my life will never be forgotten. I love you ALL so much and pray that I will be able to help, influence, love and encourage others to seek the face of Christ as you have all done for me.

Thank you to Peggy and Lloyd Hildebrand and the family at Bridge-Logos for taking a chance on me and for believing in the words that God had given me to share. Thank you to Mary Ruth Murray for editing, for praying on my behalf, and for truly caring about my well-being. Thank you to Elizabeth Nason for working with me to find a perfect cover. Thank you to Steve Becker and Shawn Myers for being the best marketing and publicity team EVER and for helping a novice like me navigate through uncharted territory.

Thank you to my agent, Tamela Hancock Murray, for representing me in the world of publishing that was initially so foreign to me and most importantly for also believing in what God had given me to share.

Thank you to Mary Busha for your hard work and editing skills, for your advice and investment in this work in so many ways, for your continued encouragement, for your unbelievable prayer support, for believing that these words will help those who are struggling and direct them back to Christ. I genuinely appreciate all that you have done for me.

Much love and blessings to you all,
Leigh-Ann

Introduction

"Praise be to God and Father of our Lord Jesus Christ, the Father of compassion and the God of all comfort, who comforts us in all our troubles, so that we can comfort those in any trouble with the comfort we ourselves have received from God. For just as the sufferings of Christ flow over into our lives, so also through Christ our comfort overflows" (2 Corinthians 1:3-5 NIV).

Today there are millions of Americans who struggle with eating disorders. Even in treatment many only learn to manage the disorder, make partial recoveries or continue to live a life of constant torment enslaved to these addictions. Most are looking in the wrong place for their answers and are continually failing at recovery. I was one of them.

After having suffered from anorexia and bulimia for nineteen years, almost loosing my life and still battling it ten years later, I was frustrated with how to find freedom from the chains of addiction that bound me. Coming up short in my recovery in hospitals, with counselors, doctors and in reading other books on the topic, I knew I had to be missing something. I was searching for victory in my battle everywhere but solely through Christ. Once I realized that He was the key to unlocking my prison door, and my walk with Him was directly connected to victory over this addiction, I was finally able to experience true freedom. I knew then that this was something I desperately needed, and wanted to, share with others who struggle in the same way.

This is the story of my personal struggle and success from anorexia and bulimia. Excerpts from my own journal provide you with a window to my heart throughout the entire process of understanding and experiencing Christ's sufficiency. Understanding my disorder, the causes and effects of addiction and searching my past were essential factors in my recovery but it wasn't until I realized the hope in God's unconditional love, His comfort in my pain, His strength to the fight the enemy and recognizing my beauty is found in reflecting His character that eventually led to true freedom from my addiction.

Everyone has a story to tell, experiences and journeys where life has taken them and how they have been affected deeply. The details of my story may be different from yours but if you are one of the millions who struggle with food then the feelings I share, the ways that I tried to cope, and the hope I was looking for, you may be able to identify with. This story of hope, recovery and reconciliation with Christ, can be found by you. You will benefit most from this book if, as you read my story, you look at your own life, can recognize the similarities and apply the foundational truths that I learned to your own walk with Christ.

The questions at the end of each chapter are designed for you to engage in your own self reflection. Because I have found lots of healing, insight, and communication with God through journal writing the questions are titled this way and are designed for you to journey with me. However, if journaling is not for you please do not feel like it is necessary to journal for recovery. I would encourage you to still use the questions for self–reflection in whatever way best suits you. They are meant to focus your self-reflection time, to dig into the cause of the initial onset of your addiction and to pinpoint trigger situations. Please don't feel like you have to stop writing or praying after you have answered them. Let God use His spirit to guide your words and heart. The Prayers provided for you at the end of the journal questions are also meant to be a guide for you to follow as you pray. They are to help facilitate your own conversation with God if you just don't know where to begin, but pray specifically as the spirit leads you. Allow the scripture verses within the text to speak to your heart, focus your mind, and work in your life. Remember, God's word is living and active.

Equally difficult to struggling through an eating disorder is the pain a loved one faces as they watch their child, spouse, or friend slip deeper into the abyss of addiction and away from a life full of health and happiness. Compiling that pain is a feeling of helplessness, frustration and fear in not knowing how to effectively support them. If you are reading this book because you are a loved one, know that there is hope. Your influence is vital in the recovery process. Portions of the manuscript were written by my husband particularly for you. With excerpts from his own journal, and collaboration on a chapter dedicated to prevention, warning signs and how to help, he shares wisdom in encouraging, loving, forgiving and supporting your loved one as well as dealing with the hurt, fear, frustration and disappointment that couples these disorders.

Hurt and pain looks differently in each of our lives, but remain at the root of addiction. What Christ has taught me, and how my life has changed from my experiences, I felt compelled to share. My heart aches for those who struggle with eating disorders and feel enslaved to food. In writing this, I hope that if you are one of the many people who struggle in that way, that you will find the keys to open your prison door as I have. If you are a parent or loved one of someone struggling with food issues my hope is that this book will better equip you to support, encourage and love them through it.

Chapter 1

How Bad Can It Get?

One percent of all adolescent girls are diagnosed
with some type of eating disorder.
Up to 20 percent of them die from it.[1]

Early one November morning in 1992, I opened my eyes to
see a nurse standing over my hospital bed. She was checking
my vital signs. She seemed confused and a bit distressed as she
repeatedly took my pulse. My hands and feet tingled. I couldn't
focus, and I felt weak. I fought to stay awake as she asked,
"How are you feeling?" I tried to respond but that required
more energy than I had at that moment. I heard her mumble,
"No, this can't be right!" Then she ran out the door and yelled
down the hallway for another nurse to come and help.

I experienced blackness, then light, then blackness again.
In my weakness, my eyes seemed unwilling to stay open. I
remember thinking, *I just want to sleep. Why won't they leave*
me alone? The next thing I knew, as I awakened yet again and
peered through my cracked lids, several doctors and nurses were
staring down at me. A bright light shone in my eyes.

One doctor kept asking me how I was feeling and if I could
focus on him. Again, I felt too tired to respond. The nurses
hurried around and said things I didn't understand. I kept
telling myself, *Leigh-Ann, wake up so you can hear what they*
are saying and answer their questions, but it was no use. All my

1

body wanted to do was sleep. My pajama top was pulled down and electric leads were placed on my chest to monitor my heart rate. All the while, the room kept fading back and forth from blackness to light.

Later, the medical staff explained to me that my heart rate had dropped to a level that caused me to slip in and out of consciousness. Once I was stable, I was helped to my feet and encouraged to walk around the room to raise my heartbeat to a safe range. I pulled out of danger quickly, and in time my heart returned to a low, but normal, rate. They monitored me for the remainder of the day until my heart rate was considered safe.

The diagnosis was that my heart had endured too much stress from the eating disorder from which I had suffered for six years. I wondered, *Where had my life gone?* No longer was it the comfortable, safe existence I once knew. I was young, just nineteen years old, and I was afraid, out of control, and sick. I had been admitted to the psychiatric floor of a local hospital a few days before. I went there by choice after my body had suffered many physical problems due to the eating disorder. I had gone down a dangerous path of destruction which I could not stop, and hit my first rock bottom.

The Downward Spiral

I had been living with this eating disorder for six years, but just prior to entering the hospital I had become completely submissive to it. I ate nothing. I would drink, but had become afraid of anything other than water and diet pop. I had begun to vomit frequently, six to eight times a day, and for long periods of time. I was trying desperately to get rid of whatever was inside. But the anger, pain, fear, sadness, and self-hatred could not be purged out no matter how much I tried. I would put food in my mouth when I was hungry and chew it up to feel the sensation of eating. Then, I would spit it out before I consumed even one morsel. I was terrified of the calories. I felt desperate to continue to purge no matter how frequently or how intense the vomiting became.

At that time, I worked at a grocery store and had begun to steal laxatives, several boxes at a time. I would swallow any number, from a few to thirty pills. The water my body retained made me feel bloated and full even though I had no food to purge. In less than a year, my body had become completely dependent on the laxatives.

I would wake up each day, strip down for a shower, and immediately weigh myself. If the number staring back at me caught me off guard, I could not handle it. Immediately, I would feel anxious and hear the words, "You've failed." I would check my reflection in the mirror. My profile had to pass the test. If my stomach was not sunken in, but rather flat or extended at all, I vomited until I felt thin enough to begin my day or the number on the scale changed. This process could take up to an hour or more.

Sometimes I would completely miss my first college class, or not go to school at all, because I couldn't leave the house looking as big as I felt I did. I weighed myself several times throughout the day. Anytime I went into the bathroom or had the urge to know how much I weighed, I would step on the scale to check the numbers.

Physically, things began to happen to me. My menstrual periods stopped. I experienced extreme abdominal pain most of the time from the laxative abuse. My bowels never worked normally. I was either constipated or experiencing horrible diarrhea. My hair began to fall out in clumps. When I washed or blew it dry, large amounts would fall out into my hands or hairbrush. I learned to style my hair in such a way to hide the mess that was happening to me.

My body couldn't take the abuse anymore. One afternoon at work, I had just purged and come back to the front of the store from my break. While I was checking out a customer, I began to feel nauseated and weak. It became difficult to focus.

I tried to continue to check her out as if everything was fine, but I could no longer see the keys on the register. There was blackness, then light. Several moments later I woke up confused. Another cashier said, "Leigh-Ann, you fainted."

A Trip to the ER

The paramedics arrived as I began to regain consciousness. They gave me oxygen and took me to the hospital. In the back of the ambulance, they questioned me about my eating and started me on an IV. I went through two bags of saline water and started on a third just to bring my body back to normal from the dehydration.

Once inside the hospital, I convinced the emergency room doctor that I would be fine. He had no idea of the extent of my addiction, which I found ludicrous, as I sat there thin and pale. He eventually released me to my parents.

My mom and dad were worried, of course, but I also managed to convince them that I was mostly just run down. I told them that I would try harder to get more sleep and eat better. My mother, being a nurse, was not naïve to what was happening. This was just one incident of many that she had had to deal with in the past several years. She knew I had problems eating, but I think she and my dad never realized how sick I was. A part of them probably didn't want to admit that their little girl was hurting herself this way.

I had already been in counseling for my eating disorder for almost three years at this point. I told my parents that I was making progress in my sessions with the help of my counselor, John. I know they wanted to believe me because they wanted everything to be all right with their little girl and they wanted to believe that professional help was making a difference. In many ways, it was, but this addiction still had a huge hold on me, and I was unwilling to give it up. I was unaware of how to let it go.

I went to spend a weekend with my friend Kay and her husband, Ron. Kay had been my Christian camp counselor from the time I was in the ninth grade, and in whom I had confided about my disorder six years before. She and her husband were dorm advisors at a college about an hour north of where I lived. I knew it was going to be difficult to purge in their small apartment. They would hear me. I decided that since I would not be able to purge, I wouldn't eat.

Soon after I arrived, Kay and I went for a walk around campus. She was always brutally honest with me, and I found it difficult—no, impossible—to lie to her face. She directly asked me what I thought I was doing. "Are you trying to kill yourself?" she asked. She knew, without a doubt, I was not okay. She pointed out that I looked frail, pale, thin, and sick. She mentioned how dry my hair had become and even noticed the areas that I had been trying to cover up. She looked in my eyes and said they looked hollow and sunken. She asked how long it had been since I had my period. I felt a lump in my throat, swallowed hard, and confessed that it had been several months. With tears in her eyes, she said that she was afraid for me.

I looked at the fear in her face and felt it in my heart a thousand times over. Then, it just came out. My mouth opened and out poured the words, "I'm scared, too." I began to cry and said that, obviously, I needed more help than I thought. She said that I needed to be hospitalized and would tell my counselor if I didn't.

In my session with John a few days later, I confessed all that I was doing. I admitted that in the past I always felt as though I could take control and stop if I wanted to. But I couldn't, and it had begun to physically affect my body. The following morning I went with my mother and admitted myself into the psychiatric floor of our local hospital.

Deception Amidst Recovery

A nurse met us as we got off the elevator. She took my bags and escorted us into a small conference-type room. She suggested that my mother leave so that I would be honest in answering my questions, but I asked my mom to stay. As we began to talk about the extent of my disorder, tears welled up in my mother's eyes. I knew what I was saying was hurting her, disappointing her, and scaring her, so I asked her to leave for the remainder of the interview.

My bags were searched right away. The several boxes of laxatives I had tried to hide between my underwear in the zipped pocket were taken from me, and I felt powerless. The nurse took me into an examining room where she and a doctor gave me a physical. I had to step on the scale with my back turned against the numbers. They wouldn't tell me what I weighed no matter how much I begged and pleaded. The nurse and resident doctor checked my vital signs; they looked in my eyes and at my hair. They made comments about how pretty I was and how I was affecting that now. Their words irritated me. I kept wondering why they thought I was pretty when I felt fat and ugly, and I wondered how much more of my hair would fall out.

After the physical, the nurse took me into the room where my mother had been waiting. She continued by explaining the daily schedule. I looked at my mother and began to cry. I was no longer in my safe place at home or in my comfortable bed with my big overstuffed teddy bear. I was in a cold, sterile, and scary place where I would be forced to eat and not be able to purge. The nurse checked my room assignment and said that there must be some mistake. I had been put in a room with a bathroom.

What luck, I thought. The nurse was trying to change my room assignment, but the floor was full. I talked the talk and told her that I was there because I chose to be; I wanted to get better and would not do anything to jeopardize that. I assured her that I would not be purging. All of that, of course, was a lie.

Inside, I felt victorious. She allowed me to stay in the room on a trial basis. This, obviously, was fine with me. I knew how to be sneaky and secretive. On one hand, I did want to get better. I was scared of what was physically happening to my body, but at the same time, I was terrified to give up my control.

My hospital days were busy. Once a day, I met with the psychiatrist assigned to me, and his team. I had to attend group and occupational therapy, meet with a dietician, work with a primary nurse, and attend classes that were designed to help patients deal with the problems in their lives. There were several classes to choose from; we had to attend two a day.

Mealtimes were the worst three parts of the day. At first I wouldn't eat. A nurse sat with me at every meal until I gave in and took my first bite. They were long mealtimes, sometimes running into the next one. After I graduated from the babysitting nurse, I was required at each meal to eat more and record what I had consumed. Many times, I would lie about what I had eaten, but they always knew. Sure, I wanted to get better, but I was terrified of letting go of what gave me comfort. It was familiar to lie and hide in order to remain in control. The doctors, nurses, and therapists watched without me knowing and questioned me when I lied to them. I felt invaded. I wanted to eat, or not eat, without their "hawk eyes" watching every move I made.

Slowly I began to gain weight. I knew because I felt bloated. My stomach was large and distended since I was not used to eating normally. Eventually that would go away as my metabolism rate regulated, but I still felt big. They weighed me once a day, but never told me what the number was. Every time someone new weighed me I tried to step on the scale so I could see the numbers, hoping they were unaware that was a restriction. They all knew why I was there and why I had to turn my back when I got weighed. My thin, frail body was evidence of that, but I felt desperate to know what that number was.

I loved having the bathroom in my room. That mistake had granted me continued control. As I gained weight, I vomited

7

more and more frequently, and as I began to eat, a part of me wanted to continue without stopping. I was so tired of being afraid to eat and so tired of feeling hungry. We ate family style at round tables, and as I watched the other patients at my table eat without hesitation, without fear, and satisfying their hunger pains, I wanted that too.

There was a kitchen area on the floor that all the patients were allowed to use. The refrigerator and cupboards were stocked with things to eat: snacks, desserts, fruits, vegetables, and more. One evening, very late, I felt like I wanted to eat. I had not eaten much at dinner and I was agitated by a conversation I had had with a nurse. I couldn't shake my hunger feeling and my desire to eat. I left my room and entered the kitchen where I found half of a chocolate cake left from lunch. I ate it all, and then went to a common bathroom down the hallway that was not used often. Since I knew that my roommate was in our room, I could not throw up there. I purged for quite some time. I felt panicked that I had just eaten so much. I vomited until a nurse knocked on the door. She had been looking for me. She knew what I was doing. I had been caught. My behavior warranted a write-up in my file, a discussion with the psychiatrist, and the topic of discussion in the next group therapy.

My Turn on the Hot Seat

I hated group therapy. I was a private person who thrived on hiding all that was inside. I never talked and I felt that it was a waste of time when others there were not dealing with the same issues I was. Because of the purging incident, I was the one on the hot seat at the next session. The group therapist questioned me about how I was feeling when I purged and what made me want to do it. I was defensive, angry, and extremely uncomfortable. I enjoyed sharing my feelings about as much as poking my eyes out. Honestly, being open with others and dealing with my feelings was treading on unfamiliar territory. I got up in the middle of the therapist's questioning and walked out of the session. Running from pain was always my typical response.

I also didn't like meeting with my psychiatrist. I thought he was cold and insincere. The nurses told him of the purging incident and the group therapist informed him of how I walked out of his session. My psychiatrist and his team believed I was playing games because I would talk about wanting to get better, but not make any progress then in my behaviors.

But I was not playing games. I was, in fact, facing an internal struggle. I didn't want to live like this. No one would. I was scared, but I didn't know how to exist without the control in my life. I wanted desperately to just talk to my counselor John. He came to visit several times to check on my progress. I wanted him to be my doctor. He already knew me and I didn't have to relive everything in my past. No matter how much I tried to avoid it, reliving my past would become a necessity for my health and a stepping-stone to my future.

Journal Questions

1. Do you feel like you have to be in control of your weight? Why or why not?

Is there a number that you must weigh in at or below? Why is that important to you?

2. Are you facing an internal struggle? What does that struggle look like in your life?

Prayer

Dear Heavenly Father,

As I continue to read this book, help me understand why controlling my weight is so important to me. Help me to follow You and feel Your comfort as I look into my past. And help me resolve my internal struggle. Amen.

CHAPTER 2

Reliving My Past

The average age of onset for anorexia nervosa is
seventeen years old. It is rare, but not unheard of,
for children under the age of ten to have the condition.[1]

" How do you think you got here?" the psychiatrist asked me. I thought that was a strange question. *He* was supposed to tell *me* that. He asked me to think about it. I had taken everything he said before with a grain of salt, but I had been asking myself this same question for quite some time. I had journaled my thoughts and feelings for many years. He asked me to consider reading my journals and contemplating his question.

My mother brought my journals the next morning. I read them all from start to finish. I started on the next clean page and wrote across the top, "How did I get here?" I began to write. As the words appeared on the page and as I searched my heart for answers, it became a journey of my life that I began to relive.

My journey begins when I asked the Lord into my life. I grew up in a Christian home and went to church every Sunday, but never understood what it meant to have a personal relationship with Jesus Christ. When I was thirteen years old, my math teacher, who was a Christian, asked me when I had accepted Christ. Naively I said, "What do you mean when? I was born a Christian. Everyone in my family is a Christian. We go to church every Sunday and are good people."

She explained to me that you aren't born a Christian and that you can't earn your way into a relationship with God by going to church every Sunday or by being a good person. She said that it wasn't even about what my family believed, but about me accepting the gift that God had given me through Jesus Christ. She went on to say that I was created by God. He was my Father. He loved me and had a plan for my life.

She told me that God is perfect and I am not. Because of that, I would always be separated from Him, so God sent His Son to die on the Cross to pay for my sins so that I could be forgiven and begin a relationship with Him that would last through eternity. All I had to do was accept Him as my Lord and Savior, and the Holy Spirit would dwell within me as a counselor and guide me in my life. She made it sound so simple. No one had ever explained it to me like that before. It was an easy decision. I sat on the edge of my bed that night, by myself, and accepted Christ into my life. It was definitely part of God's plan that we began our relationship with each other when we did. I needed Him, especially with what lay ahead of me.

The Death of a Friend

As I walked to school one cold, rainy, spring morning when I was thirteen, I felt strange, as though something was wrong, but I didn't know what. I entered the junior high building and walked down the ramp to my locker in the lower hallway. It was extremely quiet in the hallways. Nothing but a few mutters could be heard. People whispered as I walked by. Once I reached my locker, I heard someone say, "Leigh-Ann would know. Did Robby kill himself last night?" I half chuckled and said, "No! I just talked to him last night on the phone."

I turned around to find Robby's cousin staring at me. In a very quiet voice he said, "He hung himself a few hours after you talked to him." My knees felt like they were going to buckle under me and I found it hard to breathe. Tears started streaming down my face and as I started to give him a hug, one of my closest friends came running down the hallway. I started to go toward her, but then I realized she looked angry. With her finger pointing in my face, she said, "Robby is dead, and it's all because of you." Those five minutes are imbedded in my memory forever.

Robby was part of my circle of friends at school. He and I had a close friendship. We understood each other well. My other friends told me that he liked me, but I tried not to make an issue of it. I didn't want it to ruin the great friendship we had, especially since I did not reciprocate those feelings. I think for awhile I believed what my friend had said that day about it being my fault that Robby hung himself. I knew that he was facing bigger issues in his life, but I wondered if I had contributed to his heartache. For that, I felt responsible.

Sitting in the hospital that morning, I read the page in my journal dated the day I found out Robby had died.

May 7, 1987

Robby hung himself last night. We talked on the phone only a few hours before his mom found him. Was I not listening? Was he trying to tell me? Did I say something that set him off? What could it have been? Could it have been different? I keep replaying our conversation from last night over and over in my mind and I just don't understand why he felt he had no other way out. Lots of people at school are blaming me for his death. What they say is so hurtful. Don't they realize that I am grieving too? Do they think that it will make it any better to have someone to blame? Don't they know the sadness and guilt I am already feeling?

That day was quite different from any regular school day. The school had several pastors and counselors on hand if we needed to talk. I remember being asked several times if Robby was in Heaven. My friends knew that I was "religious" now, as they put it. I knew deep down that Robby didn't know the Lord, but I wanted desperately to believe that he was with Him. He knew about God and had heard me talk about Jesus. Only God knows where Robby is. It is so sad that he believed Satan's lies that his life was too horrible to live it any longer, but no one knows what happened in the last moments of his life, between him and God. I truly hope that someday I will be sitting in Heaven with Robby, praising our Lord.

The calling hours and funeral were the first I had ever been to. As I walked into the funeral home, I saw Robby's cousin throw a football to him while he lay lifeless in the casket. He said, "Get up, Robby. Let's play, *get up!*" I will never forget that scene. It was heart wrenching. As I walked up to the casket, I approached Robby's mother, introduced myself, and gave her my condolences. I said a tearful goodbye to Robby and went to sit with my friends.

A woman came over to me and said, "You are very pretty. His mother said you were his girlfriend." I replied, "Thank you, but no, I was not his girlfriend. We were just friends." I wasn't sure why his mother would say that. Maybe Robby had mentioned our friendship to her or someone from school had said something to make her think that. Whatever the reason, again I felt responsible. I had to leave. My dad had dropped me off and waited there until I was ready. I was ready sooner than I thought I would be.

Kids from school packed the funeral service, so people were standing in the aisles and up against the wall. I remember that it was so hot because of the huge crowd of people jammed into the little room where they held the service. I sat next to my friend Nicky. Emotions were high, and everyone's eyes were filled with tears as the minister gave the eulogy. Nicky was crying and as the minister began, I felt like I couldn't breathe, just like the day I found out he had taken his life. I put my head between my legs to catch my breath. As I stared at the floor, I questioned God. *Why? Why? Why did he take his life? What could have been so bad?* Mostly I wondered, *Why didn't You stop him?* In my crude, naïve way of viewing God, I blamed Him for what happened.

When it Rains, It Pours

One hot summer night three months after Robby's death, I was lying in bed, trying to fall asleep in spite of the heat. I got a telephone call from my friend Heather saying that Nicky had been in a terrible accident. Earlier that day she had been hit by a drunk driver while walking on the side of a back road. She was in horrible condition and would probably not make it. I walked out of my room to find my mom. I wanted to tell her about what had happened. I calmly told her as if I were reporting a news story. I didn't cry or allow myself to feel sad. I just went back to bed. The next day Nicky lost her fight and died. I never cried.

When the driver was prosecuted, I didn't go to court for any of the trial sessions that my friends attended. I never listened to them talking about any of the testimonies. I wanted life to go on as if the death had never happened. I would dream of Robby and Nicky being alive and very real. Then I would wake up and realize they were just dreams. The reality of it all was hard to face. I couldn't think about it. I was afraid to. I didn't think I could handle it. I was afraid that if I started to cry, I would never stop.

Once again, I found myself standing in front of a casket and saying goodbye to one of my closest friends. I wanted so badly for her just to be there, alive, not to be gone. I needed her. I still needed her in my life, and she was gone. My life continued, but I became a different person.

Inside, my anger grew. I became hard and callused. I never cried, but I never smiled. I slept, but had bad dreams. I never ate. I was depressed. My depression became anger. I felt anger toward Robby for committing suicide and toward the people in his life who had hurt him so badly that he wanted to. I was angry at the drunk driver who robbed me of more time with Nicky, but mostly I was angry at God for allowing it all to happen. I had this skewed view of God that if you were a Christian and had God on your side, then your life would be easy and full of good things, good times, and happiness. After all, He was in control of everything. I couldn't understand why He was allowing so much hurt and sadness in my life. My anger was out of control and grew with each day. The next journal entry I read was written a few days after Nicky died.

> *August 26, 1987*
> *Why does God allow life to be so unfair? Lord, why would You take Nicky so early in her life? Why would You take her from me too? I want so badly to go back in time before Robby died. I miss my friends. I am not sleeping very well. I keep dreaming about them, that they are alive. I wake up and realize I am dreaming and hope that I will fall back to sleep so that they can still be with me, if only in my dreams. When I am awake, I feel numb and in a daze. I still haven't cried. I am not sure why. My mom is worried about me.*

I wanted to be a little girl again, with no problems and no sadness. I wanted to have control of this life that was so out of control. A big part of me became obsessed with being perfect and able to handle it all. The more my life spun out of control, the more I became obsessed with wanting to be perfectly in control.

Journal Questions

1. Look up these verses: Romans 3:23, Romans 6:23, Romans 5:8, John 3:16, John 14:6, Revelation 3:20, Ephesians 2:8-9, and Hebrews 11:1. Then ask yourself the following questions: Why do I need a Savior? Why did God send His Son for me? What does Christ guarantee? What is His promise? What does it mean to be saved? How can I experience this salvation? What does it mean to have faith? What does all of this look like in my life right now?

2. Choose and finish one of the following statements, "I have a personal relationship with Jesus Christ and asked Him into my life when ..."
or
"I do not have a personal relationship with Jesus Christ and have not asked Him into my life because ..."

3. What emotion do you feel when you hear that God is in control of your life? Is there anything that you feel angry, hurt, or upset with God about? If so, what is it and what are the circumstances surrounding it?

4. Answer the following, "I don't understand why God would allow (*you fill in the blank*) to happen in my life."

Prayer

Dear Heavenly Father,
I pray You will give me the answers for whatever I am angry about, whatever I don't understand, and whatever is hurting me. Amen.

Prayer

If, at this time, you feel led to ask Jesus into your heart, you can pray this prayer to help you:

Dear Heavenly Father,

I know that You are perfect and I am not. I know the only way to have a relationship with You eternally is to accept You as my Lord and Savior. Thank You for Your sacrifice on the Cross. Thank You for Your unconditional love and forgiveness. I want You to be the Lord of my life. I believe in Your forgiveness. I believe in Your power. I believe that You paid the price for my sins. I believe in You. Forgive me for my sins, Lord; send Your Spirit into my heart, begin to work in my life, and help me to live for You. Amen.

CHAPTER 3

My Roller Coaster Ride with Food

One percent of the population suffers from anorexia nervosa. It is a drive for thinness that overpowers all other concerns and completely consumes one's life. The diagnosis includes being 15 percent below ideal body weight, an intense fear of gaining weight, a distorted body image, and the absence of three consecutive menstrual periods.[1]

I became accustomed to not eating and liked the control I had. The more I restricted eating, the more I felt in control. I lost weight quickly, and I liked that feeling. The more weight I lost, the better I felt about myself.

I ate so little, and it was easy to hide. My parents were already gone in the morning when it was time for me to eat breakfast, so I was able to skip it. For lunch, I would just eat crackers and say that I was on a diet and had had a big breakfast. In the ninth grade lunchtime was more of a social gathering anyway. We would talk with our friends, shoot baskets in the gym, or go outside to hang out until the period was over. No one really noticed what I was eating—or not eating, for that matter.

Dinner was more difficult, but I still got away with eating very little. I would move my food around my plate as if I were eating. My sister and two brothers, who were several years older than me, still lived at home, and much of the dinner conversation centered on them. I was the "baby" who blended into the woodwork, so no one noticed my eating behaviors. I would pretend to eat until everyone left the table, and then I would take my dish into the kitchen and dump the food down the drain.

My secrets and lies worked until my body could not keep up the pace without any food. One afternoon in school while I was waiting for classes to change, I was talking with a friend. I started having trouble breathing and then could not focus. The next thing I knew, I was on the floor, looking up at several students, a teacher, and the principal.

After several weeks with nothing to eat, except crackers, I had passed out in the lower hallway right outside the math room. I was embarrassed and didn't know how to get out of telling the truth. I didn't want to be taken to the hospital to be checked out, so I just told them I was fine and, in a true anorectic fashion, lied my way through the questioning. I could still see the look of concern on everyone's faces. Now, it would be more difficult to hide. I would have to start eating something at lunch for fear my teachers would tell my parents. I always had dinner at home and was questioned by my parents about what I had eaten for breakfast.

A few days of eating normally were about all I could take, however. One day after having lunch, I felt really sick. I just wanted to throw up. I got a lunch pass to the restroom and made myself vomit. A few pages over in my journal, I read about the first time I vomited.

> *March 4, 1988*
> *I threw up my lunch today. I had no choice. Everyone keeps watching what I eat. I couldn't stand for the food to be inside any longer. I had to get it out. It was kind of gross, but it felt good for my stomach to be empty again. I think I will always do that when I have to eat, as long as I can get to a bathroom.*

With that experience, I had discovered a completely new realm of controlling my weight. I also experimented with other new and dangerous methods. I used laxatives to rid my body of the food I had eaten and diet pills to control my urge to eat. I still didn't eat much, but what I did eat, I purged in some form or another.

My relationship with God at this point was distant. I never prayed and I never read the Bible. I was angry with Him for the things I was going through. He had allowed this pain in my life and I didn't know why. I felt guilty that I was hurting myself by not eating, but I still couldn't deal with the alternative—reality. I couldn't face Him.

God's Plan for Summer Camp

I grudgingly attended the youth group at my church. I was so far from God that I hated going. It just made me feel even more convicted. My mom encouraged me to attend a church camp that my cousin and a close friend had spoken highly of. I figured it would be fun with a little "Jesus stuff" thrown in. What I didn't realize is that God had bigger plans for me to be there.

The last week in July of 1988, I packed up my things to head to camp. When I got there, I met my counselor, Kay. Strangely enough, I felt comfortable with her almost from the moment I met her. She was funny, smart, extremely nice, and she seemed real, down to earth, and accepting of others. The next evening there was a short service with lots of worship. I enjoyed it immensely; however, one of the ministers began to discuss God's will for our lives and obedience to His call. It was overwhelmingly difficult to get through the rest of that service. I knew I was definitely not being obedient and I was afraid of what His will was for me since He had already allowed such hurt and sadness in my life. I broke down and started to cry.

Everything I had been trying to run away from was coming to a head. I wanted God to be in my life. I wanted Him to be in control. I wanted to follow His will for my life, but I just couldn't get past the anger and hurt of my friends' deaths and the confusion of God's place in my life. The friend who had invited me there leaned over and asked me what was wrong.

After the service, I told him everything about how I was feeling toward God and about my difficulties with eating. I told him I was scared and that I wanted to eat sometimes, but I just couldn't. He told me that I was in trouble and he needed to tell my counselor. I said, "*No way!*" I panicked. I didn't want him to tell anyone. Why did I even tell him? He walked me back to my cabin with another friend of his, and he told Kay everything. I was angry, but also relieved. I didn't want to be afraid anymore.

The Truth Comes Out

Kay and I stood outside and talked until we could not stay awake any longer. I dumped everything on her and cried and cried and cried. She told me that she would help me, somehow. That was reassuring, but also frightening. I lay awake that night staring at the bunk above me. Suddenly, I wasn't sure that I wanted help. Now that I had told her, it was no longer a secret, and I would not be able to so easily hide that I wasn't eating.

The next day we had a pizza party in our cabin. I was the only one who was not excited and did not eat. I took a piece of pizza, pulled it apart into little pieces, and moved it around my plate with a fork. I never took a bite, and almost no one noticed. Kay called me outside. *She* had noticed and said, "If I am going to help you, then you have to try. Take one bite, that's all I ask." She continued to tell me that she had never seen anyone look at their food as if worms were crawling through it.

I was terrified to eat, terrified of the food. I agreed to take one bite, but knew I would throw it up after everyone was asleep. We went back into the small cabin where the girls had already finished eating and were getting ready for bed. I took a small bite and looked over at Kay. She gave me a confirmation nod as if to say, *You did it!* I knew she felt proud of me, but inside I felt horrible. I had just eaten something and I felt horrible because I knew I was going to throw it up. As everyone else began to settle into bed, I began getting ready. I walked into the bathroom, closed the door to one of the stalls, and quietly threw up that one bite of pizza.

The next day, we left with small groups to go on two-day mission trips. Kay and I did not go on the same one. I was relieved that I could keep my secret for a few more days without someone staring at me all the time. As soon as we arrived at our destination, I located the bathrooms where it was safe for me to throw up if I needed to. Everything that I had told Kay about wanting help went right out the window.

I felt in control again and glad that she was not there. I ate enough when people were watching so they wouldn't think to ask questions, but excused myself to use the facilities after every meal. When we got back after those two days, I felt suffocated knowing that Kay would be watching me for the rest of the week. I prayed for strength, but it was just empty words. As the time neared for us to return home, I asked Kay not to tell my parents. She agreed, if I continued to be in contact with her and if I continued to try to eat.

Once I returned home, I went right back to not eating much and throwing up what I did eat. I did keep in contact with Kay. She had become a good friend and someone who cared about me. I wrote her and occasionally we talked on the phone. I lied every time she asked me how I was doing. I made her think I was doing fine, and she believed me. The more she trusted me, the easier it was to lie. I was becoming more deceptive with each day. I felt badly about that because she cared about me, but not eating had become more important.

Fooling the Doctor

During the fall of that year, I was really thin and felt horrible all the time. My stomach hurt terribly, and I felt sick more times than not. I had no energy and wanted to sleep most of the time. My mother thought something was physically wrong. She took me to the doctor who could not find anything wrong with me. I had flu-like symptoms, but no fever. He wanted to run some tests. Surprise, surprise, they came back negative. Still confused, the doctor admitted me into the hospital for more thorough tests. I did not eat. When the trays came to my room, I would dump the food down the toilet and return them empty.

After a few days of tests with negative results, my doctor caught on. He had scheduled an appointment for me to meet with the child psychiatrist while I was in the hospital. I was not happy. In fact, I was angry. When I met with the psychiatrist, she asked me lots of questions about how I was feeling and if I was anxious about eating. I had become really good at smiling through the inner fear, exuding confidence that I was fine, and hiding my behaviors. I promised them all that food was no longer an issue. I ate enough to satisfy the doctor, so I was released in a few days. My parents thought that my eating problems were no longer an issue and tucked away far into the past.

A big part of me wanted to be okay. I was tired of lying and tired of dealing with not eating when I was hungry, throwing up when I ate, and feeling sick all of the time. It was exhausting. Not eating had become the most important thing in my life. That was all I thought about: my weight, the food I ate, and how fast I could get rid of it.

I think I made several honest attempts to get better. Deep in my heart I didn't want to live like this, but I wasn't sure how not to. Now it was more than a habit, it was my security. The attempts I made to get better never lasted long. I tried hard sometimes. I would tell myself that if I wanted to eat and keep the food down I could; I just chose not to, but that was not true. It was becoming clearer to me that I was so afraid of what keeping food down would do to me, that I couldn't bring myself to do it. I was literally terrified of food. Terrified to take a bite, and if I did, terrified to leave it inside my body.

On cold mornings that winter, I would still allow myself to drink hot chocolate, made with water, as most people drink coffee. I remember the day specifically that I no longer could take a sip. I looked into that mug of hot cocoa and felt afraid. I wanted to drink it to make the inside of my body all warm and cozy before I left for school, but I just couldn't. I thought about the calories in the chocolate and then poured it down the drain. It would be several years before I would not be afraid to drink a cup of hot cocoa.

Sometimes I would talk to God about it, but I always felt that I was the one in control. Mostly, I would ask forgiveness for my actions. They were empty words. I knew He created me and loved me unconditionally, but I was telling Him I was still not good enough. About this time someone showed me Psalm 139:13-18:

> *For you created my inmost being; you knit me together in my mother's womb. I praise you because I am fearfully and wonderfully made; your works are wonderful, I know that full well. My frame was not hidden from you when I was made in the secret place. When I was woven together in the depths of the earth, your eyes saw my unformed body. All the days ordained for me were written in your book before one of them came to be. How precious to me are your thoughts O God! How vast is the sum of them! Were I to count them, they would outnumber the grains of sand. When I awake, I am still with you.*

I had such a problem with those verses and much of the whole chapter of Psalm 139. I knew that everything in the Bible was true, but to apply that to my life was more difficult. I knew He created me, but to praise Him because I was fearfully and wonderfully made was hard to imagine. I hated my reflection in the mirror. I hated what stared back at me, and I certainly did not see myself as "fearfully and wonderfully made."

Bingeing

"Fifty percent of all anorectics develop all or some symptoms of bulimia.... Three to four percent of the population suffers from bulimia. It is characterized by gorging or bingeing on food and then purging to prevent weight gain. The diagnosis includes a feeling of lack of control over eating, a minimum average of two binges a week for three months, purging and having a distorted body image."[2]

In the spring of 1989, when I was in tenth grade, I had had a really bad day at school. Several events contributed to my downcast mood that day. One specific situation affected me greatly. Now that I was at the high school, most of my teachers were unaware of my eating disorder. However, even though my thin frame was evidence of something wrong, no one really watched what I ate. I was back to crackers as a meal for lunch. On this particular day, I was sitting with my friends in the cafeteria and got up to get some water. When I came back to the table, my crackers were gone. A guy that sat with us during lunch thought it would be funny to hide them from me since I never ate anyway. When I noticed they were gone, I was furious. I yelled at everyone at the table and almost cried. I was so hungry, and someone had taken away the only thing I allowed myself to eat. I obviously overreacted. It was just a joke to them, but I was angry because the control had been taken from me.

After I got home from school that day, I was feeling really down and extremely hungry. It had been several days since I had eaten anything but crackers and a few bites at dinner. My parents were still at work, and my siblings were not at home. I felt hungry and could not shake it. I usually liked the feeling of hunger. It made me feel like I was thin and in control. That day I did not like it.

The feeling was overwhelming. I needed to eat. I grabbed a cookie and started to devour it. I grabbed another and yet another. I didn't even think about being afraid. I was too hungry. I ate the entire package of cookies. Then I looked in the refrigerator for anything I could eat. I ate pudding and applesauce and looked for more food. I ate cheese and yogurt. I finished with eating all of the bananas. I thought of all the calories and all the food I had just eaten and I panicked. Why did I do that?

I ran to the bathroom and locked the door, in case someone came home, and proceeded to vomit. I was horrified. I threw up for almost an hour, until there was nothing left to throw up. My stomach was empty, and I felt horrible. I could not believe I had just eaten so much. I knew what bingeing was, but I never thought I would do it. I always had been afraid to eat. I thought people who binged were people who couldn't stay in control and were weak. Now, I couldn't stay in control, and I was the one who was weak.

That spring I would go back and forth between not eating and bingeing. I would try not to eat, but sometimes I would binge because I couldn't deal with the hunger. I always purged. The binges became more frequent and more in quantity. The purges became more intense and, even at times, hours long. The secrets and lies became more frequent. I would steal food and laxatives. I would hide food in my closet and dresser drawers underneath my clothes. I felt victorious when I wouldn't eat the food, and I felt defeated when I devoured every last morsel of the food I was hiding.

I hid so much—food, laxatives, my behaviors—and no one knew it. I never wanted anyone to know how much food I was consuming or that I was getting rid of it. I was horrified at what I was doing. There were times that I couldn't believe how much

I was eating. I was driving now, and occasionally binged in my car, going from one fast food restaurant to another.

I was prepared with utensils, napkins to clean up with, and toothpaste and a toothbrush. Sometimes I would stop at a grocery store and buy enough food to feed several people. I would binge in my car, and then find a public restroom where it was fairly safe to purge without too many people walking in. At the worst point of my bingeing, it was hard to imagine how much I could consume. In my journal I wrote about one day specifically that I was clearly out of control.

> *October 17, 1989*
> *I had a really bad day at school today. I got a C on my math test; how could I do that? I studied so hard. I got my English paper back and some of the comments were unfair. I spent forever researching. After school I didn't come home. I felt hungry and disgusted with myself. I went to Giant Eagle and bought a half-gallon of Oreo Cookie ice cream, a container of chocolate chip cookies, potato chips, and a candy bar. I got into my car and started to eat. I drove to McDonalds, went through the drive-through and bought a hamburger, French fries, and a large drink. I drove across the street to Wendy's. There I bought a frosty and onion rings. I parked my car and ate it all. It was dinnertime, and Wendy's was busy, so I knew I couldn't throw up in the bathroom. I started freaking out about how I was going to get this food out. In the back of the parking lot, I saw a trash bin in front of a row of trees. I got out of my car and made sure I was hidden between the trash bin and the row of trees and started throwing up everything I ate. I can't believe I did that. How gross! I didn't care. I just wanted that food out of me. I have been throwing up in weird places. Sometimes I can't get to a bathroom where no one will notice me. I have been throwing up*

in the wastebasket in my bedroom and then hiding it in
the closet until I can empty it without someone seeing
me. I think I am crazy. Normal people don't do this. I
just can't stop.

It is so hard for people to realize that it is possible to eat that much at one time, but it is not about eating to fill hunger, it is about emotion to fill a need. It is both the desperation of wanting to fill an empty feeling inside and a loss of control at the same time. Food becomes an anesthetic for pain, fear, anger, or disappointment, but once the food *is* inside, panic strikes, and you realize that you have lost control and there is no choice but to purge. When the food is gone, the emptiness of pain, fear, anger, or disappointment returns, and the desperation to anesthetize with food begins again. It becomes a cycle.

It was different when I was only restricting food and had mostly anorexic tendencies. It was more of an undeserving emotion, restricting food out of a disdain for myself and wanting to remain in control. The emptiness was comforting. It meant I was in control. However, in both situations, it was a lack of feeling and true understanding of God's love for me, and the absence of a strong personal relationship with Him. I fell somewhere in between the two. I found comfort in the emptiness, but could not maintain it. When I would lose control and binge from hunger, I would try to cover up the anger inside with the food that I was eating. I did not understand God's love for me, I was angry at Him for my life being so full of pain, and my relationship with Him was definitely lacking. I did not trust Him, obey Him, or desire Him to work in my life.

There were times when I had my period off and on, and my body weight fluctuated greatly due to the bingeing, but I was still extremely thin. I continued to purge more than I binged. I felt like if I could stay one up on the food, then the calories wouldn't catch up with me.

However, I began to gain weight slowly because I was now bingeing, and eating a great deal more than normal. I felt helpless and completely out of control. I tried hard to stop, but it never lasted long—sometimes a day, a week at the most. When I would lose control, I would always starve myself until I couldn't handle it and then binge and binge and binge. It always seemed like it was worse than the time before. I never felt better. I always felt worse.

Journal Questions

1. Read Psalm 139:13-14. What do these verses mean to you? Do you believe that you are fearfully and wonderfully made? Why or why not?

2. Do you restrict food out of a disdain for yourself or as a way to please others? Or do you use food to anesthetize the way you are feeling? If so, what are the emotions you are trying to mask?

3. How does controlling your weight make you feel?

4. What are you really frightened of?

5. Journal your thoughts and feelings in moments of restriction and around moments of binges and purges.

Prayer

Dear Heavenly Father,
Help me to see myself as fearfully and wonderfully made. Help me to identify why I use food for comfort and what emotions I am really feeling that I need to address. Lord, help me not to be afraid, but rather to trust in You. Amen.

CHAPTER 4

Living the Double Life

People with eating disorders are legitimately angry, but because they seek approval and fear criticism they do not dare express that anger directly. They do not know how to express it in healthy ways. They turn it against themselves by starving or stuffing.[1]

I still attended church and youth group regularly. Late in the fall of 1989, my relationship with God began to take another turn. I began to hunger for Him. The Holy Spirit began to bring me back. Now my fear of living completely out of control began to overwhelm me, and I knew I needed God in my life. However, no matter how much fear I felt or how much I knew I needed God, I continued to hold the reins of the one area I refused to give over—my eating. I would conveniently ignore that sin. I would even pretend that my problem did not exist.

The United Methodist Church in our small town of Brimfield, Ohio, was home to about 150 people. The junior high and high school groups met together since there were so few of us. Somehow, we were left without a youth group leader. It was not a paid position, and, at the time, no one wanted to volunteer. I was the oldest in attendance, so I started to coordinate programs, socials, retreats, and lessons on my own. The pastor would oversee what I was doing, but I pretty much did it all. Regularly, we had about ten teens in attendance, give or take a few.

I planned, studied, and taught the lessons. I coordinated mission projects in the community and scheduled socials. I put together an overnight retreat in which we invited other youth groups from the area to attend. I lined up speakers and chaperones, bought the food, put up the decorations, and handled the money. I did it all.

I was the youth leader for two years. I actually thrived on the responsibility and was going to do my job with perfection. I enjoyed learning and teaching about God and the Bible, that is, as long as it didn't have anything to do with my eating. When I would study and teach, I would conveniently not relate it to that part of my life. I did, in some ways, grow closer to God during that time, but kept a comfortable, guarded distance so I wouldn't feel too guilty about hurting the creation He had made in me. I was driven to perfection more than ever, and that was where my focus stayed. I put all I had into leading the youth group and was fueled by doing a good job for the church, yet I lived in denial of the extent of my food addiction for as long as I could.

Pain on the Train

During my senior year in high school, I attended a midwinter retreat in February 1991, at the summer camp I had previously attended. Kay was the coordinator of this retreat. The theme of the event was "Celebrate Life—The Choice is Yours." Speakers talked about how bad choices had affected their lives and how these choices were not part of God's wonderful plan. The theme focused on substance abuse, abstinence, and suicide. The last, of course, was a difficult subject for me.

One speaker discussed how she was an active member of M.A.D.D. (Mother's Against Drunk Driving) because a drunk driver had killed her young child. Another talked about the dangers of promiscuity. The third speaker was a Christian counselor who spoke about a child he was counseling who had chosen to take his life in spite of the progress the counselor thought he was making. The counselor's eyes filled with tears as he talked. Clearly, that child's choice had deeply affected him.

I had such a difficult time listening to each of the speakers. The discussions in our small group were too painful for me. I just listened. Most of the people there had no idea of the tragedies I had been through years before. I probably would have been able to contribute a great deal about how my own bad choices, those of my friend, and of the drunk driver had affected my life, but I could not talk about it. It still hurt too much. It was a place I just couldn't go. I just sat there quietly, feeling like I was going to cry, but no tears came. Hiding how I felt and pretending that I was fine had become a comfortable place for me to reside.

Kay asked me periodically throughout the weekend how I was doing, and I said, "fine," "great," "okay," but I wasn't. It was hard for me to eat. I didn't want to. I consciously thought I should, but I felt sick and bloated. I didn't eat at all the whole time I was there. I played with my food and made excuses about why I didn't want to eat. I found lots of opportunities to excuse myself from the group, find the restroom with the least amount of activity, and throw up. But now there was no food to get out, only the pain and sadness I had been feeling from the weekend trip down memory lane. In some ways, I wished I could be normal and talk about my feelings, or cry when I felt I needed to, but in other ways, I knew what I had found comfort in—my eating disorders—and I was not willing to give that up.

By Saturday night, I was physically and emotionally exhausted. Not only did we rarely sleep at youth retreats, but also I was on an emotional rollercoaster, and I was not eating. By that time, I had already vomited seven times. We had an event planned late into the night. I was feeling anxious about what we were going to do next, so I went into the bathroom one last time before we started and vomited for my eighth time.

35

This activity was called the train ride. Chairs were set up two by two in a row, then an aisle and another row of two by two chairs. It was supposed to resemble the seats inside a train. The conductor, or leader, stood in the aisle as we all chose a seat. I sat somewhere in the middle on the right. The leader asked us to close our eyes and pretend with him. The train started to move. We were to look around our train. How was it decorated? What did it look like? What did we see? I saw a dark and scary train that I didn't want to be on. The walls were dingy and the seats were worn.

We were asked to look out our left window to the things of our past. What did we see that made us happy, sad, ashamed, and proud? I saw my house and myself playing in the backyard on my swing set. I saw my friends Robby and Nicky at school and then saw myself at their funerals. Then, we were asked to look out our right window to the present. What were we doing that made us happy, sad, ashamed, and proud? I saw myself standing in front of food afraid to eat. Then I saw myself eating uncontrollably and standing in front of the toilet, vomiting. I saw myself lying on the floor with stomach pains. I looked thin and sad.

The train stopped and we got out. We were to look around for a place that was safe and happy and calm. I envisioned a beach with warm sand and crashing waves, with a beautiful sunset over the water. Then he told us to look for two paths in our safe place. When looking down one, we saw light and down the other, darkness. We were to choose the path that was lit.

As we walked down the path, we met Jesus who was waiting for us. We could ask Him any question we wanted to. I asked Him why He chose to take Robby and Nicky away from me? Why did they have to go so soon? Why was there so much sadness and anger inside of me? Why did He make me the way I was? Why did I feel like the loneliest girl on the face of the Earth when I was surrounded by lots of people? Why did I hate myself? Why couldn't I just eat like a normal person? What was wrong with me? I couldn't stop with just one question. I had many.

Jesus simply replied, "Leigh-Ann, I am in control; trust and follow Me." I was so angry. That is not what I wanted to hear. That didn't answer all my questions. Maybe I wasn't listening. I turned and ran away. I ran down the path of darkness. It got harder and harder to see where I was going. It felt rough and cold and scary. I opened my eyes, got up from my seat, and ran out of the room. I was trying to make it to the bathroom. I felt like I was going to throw up. I wanted to throw up. I wanted to more than at any other time in my life.

I felt dizzy and weak. I started down the stairs. I knew this feeling. I felt it before, but kept on running. I made it down the first level to the landing and fainted on my way down to the next set of stairs. I fell down a few steps, but was caught by someone who had run after me. It was just too much. I had not slept, had not eaten all weekend, and had thrown up periodically throughout the retreat. I couldn't face what I was asked to face on that train ride—my past, my present, and my relationship with Jesus. I wanted to run away from it all.

Counseling

Monday at school was rough. I couldn't stop thinking about the weekend. I was exhausted. During my study hall, I went down to my math teacher's room to finish my homework. When I was through, I laid my head down on a desk near the register where it was warm. My eyes wouldn't close. I just sat there staring out the door into the hallway thinking of the day before.

Another teacher walked by the classroom door. I didn't notice until she came in and asked me to come with her. I followed her back to her room, wondering, *What could I have done wrong?* She sat me down by her desk and asked what was wrong with me. At first I questioned her, "What are you talking about?"

She said, "You look thin and pale." I still questioned her, and now with an attitude, "So?" but she continued to probe. She said, "Leigh-Ann, I don't know what is going on with you, but I think you are in trouble. I walked right by you and you didn't even notice me. You are here, but you're not. You look like a walking dead person. I think you are anorexic. You need counseling and I am scared for you."

I told her about the retreat. I told her how, all weekend, I felt like I was going to cry, but couldn't. I told her how I felt angry and sad, but I just couldn't talk about it, so instead I vomited. I admitted that I was scared and maybe I did need help.

I mentioned the counselor that had spoken at the retreat. I wanted to go to him. I knew he was a Christian, and I knew he cared about the kids he worked with. That was evident to me when his eyes had welled with tears at the retreat. The teacher and I walked down to the guidance counselor's office and told her some of what was going on. I told her about my eating.

The teacher who was with me said, "I told her we either had to call her parents or a counselor, and she chose a counselor." I was deathly afraid of telling my parents. How could I disappoint them, upset them like that? They would be hurt and think less of me for what I was doing. I told the teacher that I knew the counselor I wanted to go to. When I told her his name, she chuckled. John was her neighbor. That seemed so coincidental, but I knew the Lord did not work through coincidences. I knew His hand was in everything. She called John's office, but he wasn't in. She called his home and was able to reach him. He agreed to see me the next day.

No Such Thing as Coincidence

I called Kay and told her what was going on. I told her that I had not told my parents, but I didn't want to go to my appointment alone. I would be more comfortable with her because she had known John personally from church and had been the one to ask him to speak at the retreat. She agreed to go with me. That was such a difficult day. I found it hard to discuss my past with someone I did not know. He asked me some hard questions and told me to tell my parents. We set up sessions for twice a week, and so my counseling began. It would continue for the next three years, from when I was seventeen until I was almost twenty-one.

During my counseling, John asked me to do some hard things. I was still having a difficult time with anger toward Robby for taking his life and I couldn't deal with Nicky's absence in my life. I couldn't control my eating habits, and they were hurting me. I just couldn't function.

John asked me to write letters to Robby and Nicky and read them at their graves. It would be a way for me to feel like I was talking to them and that they weren't so far away. It would also be a time for me to tell them goodbye. I wrote and told Robby how angry I was at him and how selfish it was of him to take his own life. I told him that he had hurt so many people, and that he could have dealt with the things in his life that were so bad in other ways.

I walked from Robby's gravesite to where Nicky had been buried. My letter to her was quite different. There was no anger, just sadness. I missed her. As I read her letter and talked to her headstone, a woman approached. It was Nicky's mother. I couldn't believe it. That seemed so strange and so coincidental. I hadn't seen her in five years. We talked for awhile and I said it was good to see her, but I could tell she was still not doing well. I thought about that moment for many days to come. I think our meeting was probably a healing experience for both of us. I wrote about it.

May 9, 1992
I saw Nicky's mom today at the cemetery. That was strange. I can't believe it. I feel weird about that. It brings back so many memories. She doesn't seem well. I hope I am wrong. I wonder what she was thinking

when she saw me. When I told her about college, was she thinking about where Nicky would be now? Was she wondering why I am still having such a hard time with all of this? It was good to see her, but hard too. It makes me miss Nicky so much. I don't know if I can really say goodbye to her but I know I have to get past this. It has been five years. I still cannot cry.

Anger Within the Storm

My counseling sessions were tough. At some point I did grieve Nicky's loss. Finally, I was healing. I was able to see hope amidst the darkness. John told me a story, which I have never forgotten, about a pilot flying across the ocean in a storm.

The pilot was trying to get from one destination to another, but had to refuel on an island halfway between. A storm came in. The clouds made the sky dark, and the rain made visibility almost impossible. The plane was running out of fuel, and the pilot could not find the island to land on. Just when the pilot thought there was no hope left, he looked up and saw that God had provided a shaft of sunlight peering through the clouds. He followed the shaft of sunlight until it shed enough light for him to see the island. He landed safely and refueled his plane to reach his final destination.

I remembered that story when I felt helpless about my eating. When I felt there was no hope left and only darkness was ahead, I thought of that story and realized there is always hope with God. He provides all we need to get through the storm. The story reminded me of Peter in the Bible. He walked on water until he took his eyes off Jesus and looked at his circumstances. It was apparent that when I took my eyes off God, I fell deeper into my disorder. The times when my relationship with God was stronger, I was healthier. The times I wanted to be in control, it was then I was dangerously falling away. This was an easy concept to understand, but difficult to live out.

One of the most difficult parts of my counseling was dealing with my overwhelming anger. I still held tight to the anger toward the drunk driver who killed Nicky. I had only let some of the anger toward Robby go that day in the cemetery, and I was still so angry at God for all of it. I had come to the realization that the pain I caused myself with my eating disorder was a result of trying to deal with that anger.

Now that I knew I was holding on to the anger and hurting myself, I had to come up with a healthy way to release it. I told John that I felt like I wanted to throw something and watch it break. He suggested I throw eggs at a tree. My home had a large wooded area directly behind our yard. I knew that I could feasibly go there and no one would see or hear me. I picked up six dozen eggs, went out back to a private area during the middle of the day, and began to throw.

At first, I just threw a few at the tree and enjoyed watching them break, but as I kept throwing eggs the anger just overwhelmed me. I yelled and screamed at that tree and at God. I threw the eggs so hard that my arm hurt. I kept throwing until all six dozen were gone. I wanted more to throw. I still had more to get out of me. For the first time, I experienced my anger turned outward, instead of inward at myself. However, for me, that was clearly not the answer. I was still angry and now feeling aggressive. Over time, the anger and aggression lessened, but until recently I never really learned to turn toward God, seek Him for comfort and answers, and let Him take it all away from me. I needed to learn to trust God, forgive others, and not let the anger harbor inside of me.

My dear brothers, take note of this: Everyone should be quick to listen, slow to speak and slow to become angry, for man's anger does not bring about the righteous life that God desires. (James 1:19-20)

On the contrary, my anger led to sin and unrighteousness that was keeping me from my relationship with God and giving Satan another stronghold in my life.

Even though I was learning more about myself and working on my anger in counseling, I continued to live my double life. My need for perfection, control, and acceptance even manifested there. I wanted my counselor to think that I was doing well, too. I wanted to please him and please my parents with the notion that I was getting better. I continued to roller coaster with my eating. Sometimes, I really believed the lie that I was in control of this addiction, but I could only live that lie when the circumstances of my life were within my control.

Just What Is in Control?

At some point, and you don't know when it happens, the control you thought you had is gone and the disorder begins to control you.

My freshman year in college at Kent State University was difficult. I started dating someone seriously. In fact, I thought he was *the one*. We dated for not quite a full year, and I thought I was happy. When he ended the relationship at the end of the summer of 1992, I was devastated. I just could not take his rejection. I had depended upon him for my happiness. He was the one who told me I was beautiful. He made me forget my past. I was desperate to be loved and to get approval. I was completely clueless to the reality of how unhealthy this relationship was. I questioned, *What's wrong with me?*

The rejection I felt from him triggered a deeper level to my addiction. Reading the last journal entry before I had entered the hospital brought tears to my eyes.

> *October 5, 1992*
> *I don't understand why Scott doesn't want to be with me. Am I not pretty enough? Maybe I'm not thin enough? He talked about how he used to date some girl*

that was a stick. She had gone on a diet of only eating plain popcorn and water for a whole summer and he noticed how great she looked now. Well, I am not even eating that. He said I was too dependent on him, but I think that is a lie. I don't understand, God, I thought he was the one. He made me so happy. No one will ever love me. Why did you make me this way?

That journal entry was difficult to read because the pain was fresh; it was fueling my obsession with being in control of my eating. Soon after our break-up, I found myself riding in the car with my mom on my way to the hospital. I didn't know then that this car ride would lead to one of the most desperate times in my life, when my heart began to slow its beat and then lead to the beginning of thirteen years of *managing* my eating disorder and following God.

After my first week in the hospital, I was allowed out on a supervised pass with my parents. The objective was to go to my favorite restaurant with them, then come back and report how it went. It was a Saturday and no group sessions or occupational /nutritional classes were scheduled. I had a pass for the entire afternoon. I lied and told my parents that I needed to be back for a class in two hours. My roommate was also on an afternoon pass, so I knew my room would be empty, and the nurses would not know I was there.

We ate a leisurely meal at The Olive Garden Italian Restaurant. I was fearful of the food that I was eating. It took so much to eat just a few bites, but my parents were satisfied that I was at least eating something. I cut the food up and moved it around on my plate while I talked about how I was getting better and making progress, which was not true. I felt just as bad as ever, but now I had to eat and be more creative with my purges. We finished eating and soon afterward, I was back at the hospital.

My parents dropped me off; I told them I had to go because of the class I was to attend. I walked right past the nurses who had been chit-chatting in the nurse's station. A large number of patients were out on passes. The nurses never even noticed me. As I walked to my room at the end of the hall, I could still hear them talking, and I knew I hadn't been spotted. I felt a sense of relief that I could get this food out of me without anyone knowing. I closed the door behind me, went into the bathroom, and started to vomit.

This time, my feelings seemed to be more intense than ever. I was trying to hurry and started to hurt my throat more than usual. The food was not coming out fast enough. I felt desperate. I grabbed my toothbrush and shoved it down my throat as hard as I could to gag myself. I needed to get more out. I needed to keep throwing up. I don't even know how long I had been vomiting. I felt light-headed and sick. My throat hurt. My chest hurt. My stomach hurt. Everything hurt.

I lay down on the floor beside the toilet, held my stomach, and began to cry. I was not getting better. I was feeling more scared and desperate than ever. My roommate, Betsy, came into the room and heard crying from inside the bathroom. The door was locked, so she knocked. I replied that I was fine. She said, "Let me in or I will call the nurse." I reached up from the floor and unlocked the door. She came in and wrapped her arms around me. She said, "You have to stop. You are going to kill yourself."

Betsy had a son at home and talked of him often. She asked me if I wanted to ever have children. I wanted a family more than anything in the world. She looked at me with tears in her eyes and said, "Leigh-Ann, you will never know what that is like if you keep on hurting yourself this way." I felt the reality of that more than ever, especially since I had not had my period in several months.

The next morning my heart began its slow and irregular beat, and I knew Betsy was right. As the doctors and nurses watched me that day, checking my vital signs frequently and never letting me out of sight, I knew things had to change. I needed God. I could not fight this on my own any longer and expect to win. I had been trying for six years. That night I sat on the edge of my bed in the dark and prayed like I had never prayed before. I addressed all that I had been trying to hide from God in the past. I had never let Him into that area of my life and now I was laying it at His feet. I confessed my sin, and I broke. I said, "Lord, this being in control of my life thing ... it's not working, and I need You to be the Lord of my life again." I needed Him and finally allowed Him to take control of my life. It was at that moment I truly began a whole and honest relationship with God.

Journal Questions

1. Who is it that you are afraid to fail or are trying to please?

Finish the sentence, "I feel like I need to be perfect because ..."

2. What would happen if you failed or were not seen as "perfect" or "having it all together?"

3. How are you affected by rejection from others?

4. If it were you on that train ride, how would your train look?

5. What would you see out of the window of your past that makes you happy, sad, ashamed, or proud? What would you see out of the window of your present that makes you happy, sad, ashamed, or proud?

6. Finish the sentences:

"My safe place looks like ..."

"If I were to meet Jesus, I would ask Him ..."

7. Read James 1:19-20. Where is your anger or pain leading you?

Prayer

Dear Heavenly Father,

Help me to see the things in my life that have brought me to this point. Help me recognize that You are always there for me, and help me face those issues that I have been running from. Amen.

CHAPTER 5

Understanding My Disorder

"Overeating and excessive dieting both increase a woman's health risks, but the effects become more life-threatening when preoccupation turns to disorder."
– Dr. Lesley Hickin[1]

My therapy began to change. I went from hating every moment to actually listening to what the professionals helping me had to say. My attitude toward the therapists, nurses, and doctors did a complete turnaround. I worked with the primary nurse who taught me a great deal about the dangers of eating disorders. The occupational therapist worked with me on body image and self-esteem. I worked with a dietician who came up with a diet that would promote eating enough calories for my body. I continued with group therapy, where the support of my roommate and the woman across the hall was encouraging. I also continued therapy with my psychiatrist who oversaw all of my therapy.

My relationship with Joyce, the primary nurse working with me, grew stronger as she taught me about my eating disorder. She first explained to me that I was not alone and that there were several thousands of women and some men who struggle with eating disorders every day. She told me about my disorder specifically. She said that I contained characteristics of both *anorexia nervosa* and *bulimia nervosa*. We talked of those characteristics.

She told me that anorexia is characterized by obsessive concern with food and weight, which continues even after one has become thin; a distorted and irrational view of self, by talking about being fat when, in reality, already exceedingly thin; fear of food or gaining weight; rigid ritualistic eating patterns, such as limited ingestion of food or chewing up food and spitting it out without swallowing; and cooking large lavish meals for others, but not partaking in them. It is also characterized by rigid ritualistic or compulsive exercise habits, repeatedly checking weight or significant weight loss, hiding weight loss, obsession with examining self in mirror, loss of menstrual periods, water retention, constipation, feeling cold, wearing big baggy clothes to stay warm, hiding the weight loss, and a fear of food. These behaviors can be coupled with fainting, weakness, and exhaustion, as well as depression and anxiety.

The clinical diagnosis for anorexia is being "15 percent below ideal body weight, an intense fear of gaining weight, a distorted body image, and the absence of three consecutive menstrual periods."[2]

She said that bulimia is characterized by bingeing (rapid consumption of large amounts of food or eating when not hungry and being unable to stop), purging (self-induced vomiting, laxative abuse, dieting, or restrictive behavior after a binge), and secretive behavior such as hiding or hoarding food, disappearance after meals, hiding laxatives, or the like. It is common to see swollen glands, a puffy face, have feelings of weakness, dizziness, and hand sores or calluses. Nothing she said was foreign to me.

The clinical diagnosis for bulimia includes "a feeling of lack of control over eating, a minimum average of two binges a week for three months, purging and having a distorted body image."[3]

This is a good time to note that whether you fit the criteria for a clinical diagnosis or not, you may still have an eating disorder. If you can identify with, or are engaged in, several of the above behaviors, there is a problem that you must address before it snowballs into something bigger or affects you spiritually, physically, and emotionally more than it already has. Eating disorder behaviors are addictive and become footholds for the enemy that, if left unaddressed, can spiral into something that controls you and every area of your life. Do not be deceived by the idea that you are still in control and you will stop before it gets worse. That is deception from the enemy. It will take control before you are able to realize it. What starts as a behavior easily becomes a habit and a habit that easily becomes an addiction.

Joyce told me that both anorexia and bulimia, because of poor nutrition, affect physical appearance. Lack of food manifests itself in dry skin that looks gray in color, brittle nails that break and split, and eyes that look bloodshot, sunken in, and glossed over. Because of vomiting, teeth rot, enamel erodes, and gums recede; bloating and water retention occurs from laxative abuse. Hair is affected greatly. It will become extremely dry and sometimes fall out. In extreme cases of anorexia with a significant weight loss, some may experience hair growth on their bodies called *lanugo*. She told me that our body is designed to protect us, and when it does not contain enough fat reserves to keep us warm, actual hair will grow on the body to maintain body temperature. I had experienced many of these same effects to my physical appearance, including finding out several months after my stay in the hospital that my gums had severely receded.

Joyce and I also talked of the similarities and differences between the two disorders. She explained that both are characterized by excessive concern with food and weight and those afflicted take excessive measures for weight control. Both anorexics and bulimics have underlying issues of hurt and pain and have unrealistically high self-expectations. However, there are significant differences as well.

An anorexic denies that she has a problem where a bulimic recognizes her abnormal eating patterns. An anorexic will show significant weight loss, where a bulimic will tend to be ten to fifteen pounds within her weight range. An anorexic likely will be socially withdrawn while a bulimic will tend to be very outgoing. An anorexic will have rigid control over her eating and turn away from food to cope. A bulimic will show a loss of control over her eating and turn toward food to cope. Joyce stressed that it is important to note that eating disorders are, in fact, coping mechanisms for underlying issues of hurt and pain.

Physical Appearance Affected by Poor Nutrition
- Dry skin with grayish color
- Brittle nails that break and split
- Eyes are:
    Sunken
    Glossed over
    Bloodshot
- From vomiting and acid build-up:
    Teeth rot
    Enamel erodes
    Gums recede
- From laxative abuse:
    Bloating and water retention occur
- Hair becomes dry, develops split ends, and may fall out
- Body hair growth (lanugo) in extreme cases of anorexia

Similarities
Both bulimics and anorexics have excessive concerns with food and weight.

Both take excessive measures for weight control.

Both have unrealistically high self-expectations.

Differences

<u>**Bulimics**</u>   <u>**Anorexics**</u>

Bulimics	Anorexics
1. Recognizes abnormal eating	Denies problem
2. Tends to be ten to fifteen pounds within weight range (15 percent below ideal weight)	Shows significant weight loss
3. Loss of control of eating	Rigid control of eating
4. Turns toward food to cope	Turns away from food to cope
5. May be socially outgoing	May be socially withdrawn

Medical Effects

Joyce warned me of the outcomes from the dangerous methods of purging. Syrup of ipecac is a drug that is used to induce vomiting and is used mainly when a toxin is ingested. Abuse of this drug can cause a weakened heart muscle, irregular heartbeats, chest pain, breathing problems, and cardiac arrest, which is the main cause of death in bulimics.

Laxatives are drugs that trigger the bowel to work when someone is constipated. Abuse of this drug can cause diarrhea, bloody diarrhea, dehydration, severe abdominal pain, internal organ damage to the colon and liver, and an imbalance of electrolytes, which maintain proper functioning of muscles, nerves, and vital organs. In truth, laxatives have little or no effect on weight loss because by the time they begin to work, calories have already been absorbed. All that really happens is a loss of water that the body is retaining.

Serious results of laxative abuse to your body according to Anorexia Nervosa and Related Disorders, Inc. are:

• You can upset your electrolyte balance. Electrolytes are minerals like sodium and potassium that are dissolved in the blood and other body fluids. They must be present in very specific amounts and exact ratios for proper functioning of nerves and muscles, including the heart muscle.

• Laxatives and enemas (and also forced vomiting) can upset this balance by flushing essential minerals out of the body, resulting in muscle cramps, tremors, spasms, irregular heartbeat, and in some cases cardiac arrest. The heart stops, and unless the person receives immediate emergency medical treatment, she dies.

• Laxatives and enemas (and also vomiting) remove needed fluid from the body. The resulting dehydration can lead to tremors, weakness, blurry vision, fainting spells, kidney damage, and in some cases, death. Severe dehydration requires medical treatment. Drinking fluid may not hydrate cells and tissues quickly enough to prevent organ damage or death.

• Laxatives irritate intestinal nerve endings, which in turn stimulate muscle contractions that move the irritant through the gut and out of the body. After a while the nerve endings no longer respond to stimulation. The person must now take greater and greater amounts of laxatives to produce bowel movements. She or he has become laxative dependent and without artificial stimulation may not have any bowel movements at all.

• Laxatives and enemas strip away protective mucus that lines the colon, leaving it vulnerable to infection.

• Enemas can stretch the colon, which over time becomes a limp sack with no muscle tone. No longer can it generate the muscle contractions necessary to move fecal matter out of the body.

• Laxatives abusers seem to have more trouble with the following problems than do nonusers: irritable bowel syndrome (rectal pain, gas, and episodes of constipation and diarrhea) and bowel tumors (both benign and cancerous).[4]

Laxative abuse causes an addictive cycle because when fluids are expelled, they leave an empty feeling, but within forty-eight hours, the body begins to retain an equal amount to the water that was lost. This produces a bloated feeling and leads back to use of the laxatives. Then the cycle begins again.

Diuretics or water pills have many of the same effects as laxatives. Diet pills contain stimulants and caffeine that affect the central nervous system. This causes increased heart rate, dizziness, elevated blood pressure, nausea, anxiety, insomnia, dry mouth, and diarrhea. Some diet pills contain the stimulant ephedrine, which has been known to cause heart attacks, seizures, and strokes. Self-induced vomiting can tear and rupture the esophagus, cause chronic hoarseness and sore throats, choking, dizziness, fainting, chest pain, and irregular heartbeat.

Joyce continued to tell me about further medical complications due to eating disorders. She told me that poor nutrition leads to muscle wasting, a loss of bone mass, and osteoporosis. There is also lowered strength and stamina, insomnia, headaches, and a lowered red-blood cell count that can cause anemia. Low potassium can lead to nocturnal cardiac arrest. When starvation occurs, the metabolic rate is lowered and the body burns calories at a slower pace. Shortness of breath, irregular heartbeats, convulsions, and low blood pressure are all effects of strain on the heart. Electrolyte imbalances lead to ovary failure and infertility, liver damage, kidney failure, and cardiac arrest.

As she informed me of the medical problems, I listened intently and realized that many of them were all too familiar. I knew I did not want to experience any more than I already had. It scared me to know how much I was hurting my body and how much harm can occur from an eating disorder.

If you are binging and purging, taking laxatives, or have been starving yourself, I highly suggest you go to your family doctor and have a complete physical. There is so much that can be happening inside your body from lack of nutrition and purging that you may be unaware of until it is too late.

Common Causes

As I worked with the psychiatrist, I learned more about the causes of eating disorders and why they manifest in girls who have had similar backgrounds. The psychological cause deals mainly with a love hunger, perfectionism to gain approval, and a need for control in their lives. It is a coping mechanism for other larger issues at hand. Primarily, it is a way for that person to feel in control of something and to seek approval from others. The circumstances of each person who suffers from eating disorders may vary greatly, but the feelings and emotions that manifest from those circumstances are quite similar.

The family upbringing can be a significant factor. "Relatives of individuals who have had eating disorders are seven to twelve times more likely to develop anorexia or bulimia than relatives of individuals who have never had an eating disorder."[5]

There is current research to show there may be genetic influences in the development of eating disorders, but family influence can be a significant factor in its onset as well. Typically, eating habits are formed by the examples of eating patterns within the family and by the amount of focus put on body image and self-esteem. Sibling competition or teasing, parent personality and discipline, and/or spousal influence can have a lasting effect on the way we view ourselves and how we react to rejection. Characteristics commonly found in the mother of someone suffering from an eating disorder are that of one overly involved in her child's life and one who avoids conflict. Characteristics commonly found in the father tend to be over-protectiveness, rigidness, and controlling behavior, yet maintaining an emotional distance. He typically stresses perfection and has excessively high expectations for his child. While these characteristics are common, they are not true in every case.

The personality of the person who has the disorder is also part of the equation. Eating disorders are generally found in girls, so for purposes here I will refer to someone who suffers from an eating disorder as "she." She usually has low self-esteem and difficulty with accurate observations of self. She is usually a people-pleaser to gain approval from others and has a desire for control in her life. Often she is a compliant, model child who is sometimes compulsive, but always a perfectionist. She has excessively high and unrealistic self-expectations. She also has a desire for social acceptance as her body changes through puberty. This is typically why so many eating disorders begin in adolescence. She hungers for the love and attention that she may not be getting at home, and she can't cope with criticism or emotionally deal with hurt and disappointment in her life. Typically, control of food becomes her coping mechanism.

The societal influences in America also contribute to the way girls view themselves when they are growing up. There has been such an emphasis on outer beauty and thinness in our country that little girls are growing up with the pressure to be a size zero in order to feel good about whom they are. Pictures of models and celebrities are all over television. They are on billboards and in magazines. Girls grow up thinking that these emaciated women are the standard for beauty. The truth is, several models and actresses have revealed their difficulties with eating disorders while trying to maintain this unrealistic standard of beauty. Girls are desperately trying to look like the model images they see, and the reality is that because of their body types, they may never be able to be that thin and still be healthy.

We live in a society where women in beauty pageants, models, and Barbie dolls are images of beauty. Beauty pageants place a huge emphasis on body image. The message again is that beauty depends mostly on outer appearance. Women compete to be declared the most beautiful. Barbie dolls have also caused problems with regard to the images that girls are receiving. They grow up thinking that this is what an adult woman looks like. The expectation is that when they grow up, they will look like Barbie. The reality is that the proportions on a Barbie doll are impossible. No real woman could have the same proportionate dimensions as Barbie's body measurements.

Plastic surgery today is acceptable and encouraged for the sole purpose of making yourself more beautiful. Here the message is that if you don't like something about yourself, God must have made a mistake when designing you. Go ahead, change it. It will make you feel better about who you are and boost your self-esteem. There have been several plastic surgery makeover television shows that convey the message that beauty is about how you look, and if you are *beautiful*, you will have a better self-image. We need to ask ourselves, "What are we seeing, buying into, and teaching our children?" Many women in the entertainment business have also suffered from eating disorders. We see it all the time in Hollywood. Some have not yet admitted to having eating disorders, but we can see the evidence in their emaciated bodies and know they are unhealthy. However, there are others who have confirmed the struggle they have faced with being in the public eye and feeling a need to be perfect. Stars such as Tracy Gold from *Growing Pains* and Jamie Lynn Sigler from *The Soprano's* have suffered from anorexia. Singer Karen Carpenter eventually lost her life to it. Paula Abdul and Katharine McPhee both have suffered from bulimia, but have reportedly sought help. There have been athletes who have suffered from issues with eating as well. Gymnast Christy Henrich's anorexia proved to be fatal in 1998.

Outer versus Inner Appearance

The occupational therapist also worked with me on my self-image. She said that it was important for me to remember that my exterior was just the shell that housed who I really was. She asked me if it was important to me for others to see what kind of person I was. It was, but it was also important to me for others to see someone who was perfectly in control. Sarah was also a Christian, so we talked of wanting others to see Jesus in me. I did want others to see a pure heart with righteous intentions. I wanted my focus to glorify God, and my life at this point was not exemplifying that. She shared with me a quote from Marcia Hutchinson that said, "Your body is where you'll be living for the rest of your life; isn't it time you made it your home?"[6] I needed to make my body my home.

Food and Nutrition

The last area of my treatment was working with a nutritionist. She taught me about food and nutrition, and set up a meal plan for me to eat normally including the number of calories my body needed to stay healthy. I used that plan for quite some time and it was helpful in managing my disorder. I found, however, that it too was restrictive, and it did not teach me how to eat within God's will and listen to my body's cues for the healthy nourishment it needed.

The individuals on the team that worked with me in the hospital were wonderfully dedicated professionals who truly wanted to see me healthy. The information I gained from being there was helpful in managing my disorder for many years without full relapse into the addiction.

Journal Questions

1. Does the concern you have for food and weight consume your thoughts?

2. What are the expectations you have for your weight and for your life?

3. What ritualistic behaviors with food or exercise need to be a part of your daily routine?

4. Do you find yourself covering up, hiding, or lying so that others will not ask about your weight loss, abnormal eating habits, or frequent trips to the bathroom?

5. Are there certain foods that you consider "forbidden" or foods that are "safe"? What are they?

6. Is binging or purging a way you control your weight and cope with stress? Do you have behaviors of self-induced vomiting, over-exercising, or laxative abuse? If so, how often are you vomiting and over-exercising and how many laxatives are you taking? Does this seem more excessive than the norm?

7. Look back into the chapter at the chart on physical appearance affected by poor nutrition. Look in a mirror. How is your appearance being affected by your eating habits?

8. Do you turn away from food or toward food to deal with stress or anxiety in your life? In what ways?

9. What is happening to your body right now because of the way you are treating it?

10. How have the influences of the people in your life (parents, siblings, spouse, or friends) affected the way you eat? With what characteristics can you identify in someone who struggles with an eating disorder? How have images in the media affected the way you view yourself?

Prayer

Dear Heavenly Father,

Help me to see if my eating patterns are indicative of an eating disorder, and help me to have confidence to confide in someone I trust for help whether that person is a counselor, parent, or good friend who has authority and influence in my life. Help me to see the significant impact my eating patterns can have on my health and then to honestly see how these are affecting me. Amen.

CHAPTER 6

Sharing What I Knew

My speaking was beneficial in two ways. First, I felt that God had called me to use my experience in a positive way so that other girls would not struggle as I had. Second, it kept me accountable.

I had learned so much from my time in the hospital. I learned about myself and about how much I had jeopardized my life. I sat on the edge of my hospital bed the evening after my heart's beating had slowed and prayed in a way that I had never before. I repented and asked the Lord to help me stay strong. I told Him that trying to be in control just wasn't working and I needed Him to be the Lord of my life again. I made a commitment to take care of myself so that I could experience the life the Lord had intended for me.

For awhile, every day was a battle to stay healthy. Every meal and every bite was a challenge to take and a challenge to keep down. It was baby steps of faith that got me through the rough times. I was scared and didn't want to live like that anymore.

The closer I grew to the Lord, the easier it was for me to stay healthy. The days that had seemed so challenging started to go by without any fear of eating. Soon a week went by, then two and three. Months became easier as well. I finally realized the importance of having a personal relationship with Jesus Christ and being an example for Him. I wanted to make a difference and help others who were struggling with eating disorders.

I went back to that same high school teacher that had been there for me two years earlier and shared my desire to talk to other girls who might be in danger of experiencing eating disorders. She asked me to come in that Friday and speak to her whole class. The opportunity I wanted was staring me in the face and I was petrified. Since our school was so small, these were people I knew. I wasn't sure that I wanted to share all I'd experienced with people I had gone to school with. But when I thought about girls secretly dieting or bingeing and purging, then there was no question in my mind.

Friday came sooner then I wanted. I went into the classroom trembling. I looked around and saw familiar faces. In fact, I knew just about everyone in there. I began to talk about what eating disorders are and specifically about anorexia and bulimia. I talked about the dangers of poor nutrition. I shared what I had learned while I was in the hospital. As I began to tell my story, all eyes were focused on me. I could hardly swallow, but continued to share my struggles with food, dieting, bingeing, and purging for the past six years.

When I finished my talk, they asked me questions until the bell to dismiss them interrupted us. Three girls stayed after class to talk with me about their own difficulties with food. I stayed there for the next hour trying to instill in them the beauty and worth they possessed and the insanity of bingeing and purging or starving themselves. My emotions overwhelmed me. I was relieved that it was over, but I was extremely concerned with the well-being of these three girls. I felt good knowing that what I said would be on their minds the next time they wanted to harm themselves. I directed them to the school counselor and gave them numerous ideas to help keep them on track.

I kept in close contact with those three girls for quite some time. One girl began to eat normally again on her own. She had only dabbled in what it would be like to binge and purge, but did not want to risk her future health. The other two girls seemed serious about losing weight and entered into counseling.

The Lord opened the floodgates from that point on. The word spread about the talk I gave. I was invited to speak four more times that month. Soon other schools called me to talk in their fitness, nutrition, and cooking classes. Then I began speaking in personal development, family living, and similar classes. I spoke at least two to three times a week in several different schools, college campuses, and church youth groups. I kept up the pace and continued with my college classes. I felt that as long as there was a need and God provided the opportunities, then I would continue to speak. I spoke on a regular basis for five years.

My speaking was beneficial in two ways. First, I felt that God had called me to use my experience in a positive way so that other girls would not struggle as I had. Second, it kept me accountable. As long as I stood up in front of a group of people and told them that I was healthy, I had to be healthy. I would not be any help to anyone if I did not believe and live what I was saying.

Shortly after I had started speaking, Kent State University ran an article about me in their campus newspaper, *The Kent Stater.* I was a student there, but I also spoke on campus. My friend Kristen, who read the article and remembered me from many years ago at church camp, invited me to a Christmas party for Campus Crusade for Christ. I went, loved it, and signed up for a Bible study on campus. I grew a great deal spiritually from that study. I learned about sharing my faith and applying biblical truths to my life. I was a broken person now, but becoming renewed, refreshed, and whole.

It was there, at the Christmas party, that I met a man who had an incredible heart for God. His personality was magnetic. People were drawn to Todd. The first night we met, we talked for hours. His love for the Lord was so evident. We began to date, and it was not long before I knew that Todd was the one God had intended for me.

God had done a major work in my life prior to this point. Soon I realized that He had brought me to a place of health and prepared me to begin my life with Todd. On June 29, 1996, Todd and I were married. He has continued to be a source of strength and support in my life. He is my best friend, a huge encouragement and support, and the love of my life.

I had told Todd early on in our dating relationship about my eating disorder, how severe it had become and about my visit to the hospital where God had brought me back to Him. Todd's reaction was wonderful. He said that we all have things from our past that Satan wants to use to keep us from experiencing the true forgiveness that God offers. I remember that discussion vividly because then he added, "You are a new creation in Christ and His forgiveness is unconditional. What has happened in your past is in the past and does not affect or change how I feel about you now or make me respect you any less." Todd is an amazing man who truly knows how to forgive and love unconditionally. This trait of Christ in Todd is what helped to build the foundation of our marriage during our first year and what has kept us strong through the storms.

One month before our first anniversary, we found out that I was pregnant. Although we were surprised, we were also so excited and thankful. I wanted children desperately, and I knew it was truly a gift from God. With all that I had put my body through, I wasn't even sure that I could conceive and carry a child. What a blessing from God and a victory for me! Nine months later, a beautiful baby girl entered our lives. We named her Emily Faith. Her middle name, Faith, was given as a testimony of God's faithfulness in our lives. Little did I realize then that God would teach me much more about His faithfulness in the years to come.

After my baby was born, I struggled with the weight that I had gained—fifty-two pounds in all. During my pregnancy, I was afraid to deny myself anything because I wanted to make sure this child, who was dependent on me, would be healthy and lack nothing. I didn't know how to eat properly, which I used as an excuse to eat whatever I wanted. I looked so different and my body felt strange to be so much heavier. After Emily was born, I battled feelings of being fat and the reality of not fitting into my jeans. Satan took the opportunity to tempt me several times, but every time I looked into my baby girl's eyes, the Lord reminded me of His faithfulness and grace. I felt that I did not deserve to have her because of all I had done to my body, but the Lord had blessed me anyway.

Two years later, I found that I was pregnant again. What a joyful gift God had given us, but again Satan tried to tempt me. With the weight gain, grew anxiety. As my clothes began to fit snugly and the numbers increased on the scale, my feelings of fear reappeared. My second child, Christopher Todd, was born November 11, 2000. He was a big boy and had stretched my body to its fullest capacity. During this pregnancy I, again, denied myself nothing and gained a great deal of weight. After Christopher's birth, I found it extremely difficult to get my body back to where it had been before the two pregnancies. I was frustrated with the changes in my body even though it was evidence of my two beautiful children. Somehow, I managed to get through for three more years.

During that time, I lived in fear of returning to the eating disorders of my past because now I was responsible for two young children. I tried to pretend that food was not an issue, but deep down it still was. I ignored the weight gain, as if it didn't bother me, and ate whatever I wanted, even if I wasn't making good choices. My life had become full of blessings and wonderful things, and I remained focused on that. I didn't feel the need to be in control as much, but I still didn't know how to eat healthy.

Journal Questions

1. What times in your life have your eating patterns seemed more out of control?

2. What is the common denominator in those situations? Is there a reoccurring pattern or emotion? Can you pinpoint trigger situations, discussions, or emotions? What are they?

3. When does Satan seem to tempt you most and expect that you will fall?

Prayer

Dear Heavenly Father,

Help me to see the pattern of abnormal eating in my life. Help me to see when I am the most vulnerable against the temptation of this food addiction. Help me to seek You for refuge and strength. Amen.

CHAPTER 7

Wayward Again

*Even 40 percent of those who are in treatment for eating disorders
fail to make full recoveries. Twenty percent only make partial
recoveries and 20 percent are still living a life tormented by
addiction of food and weight.*[1]

OLord, do not rebuke me in your anger or discipline me in
your wrath. Be merciful to me, Lord, for I am faint; O Lord,
heal me, for my bones are in agony. My soul is in anguish. How
long, O Lord, how long? Turn, O Lord, and deliver me; save
me because of your unfailing love. No one remembers you
when he is dead. Who praises you from the grave? I am worn
out from groaning; all night long I flood my bed with weeping
and drench my couch with tears. (Psalm 6:1-6)

Our church had a woman's retreat focusing on trust in
April of 2003. On the car ride there, I was telling my friend
what I thought the Lord was going to work on in me while I
was there. I had some issues about trusting Him with finding
us a new home. The retreat was amazing and eye-opening for
me in many ways. We had great fellowship, the message was
incredible, and we had some significant time to journal. As I
wrote, it was clear that I had deeper trust issues with God than I
had realized. I found that I still had many areas in my life that I
felt I had to control. As hard as I tried to give things over to the
Lord, I would always choose some area in my life to continue

to manage. During the entire retreat I felt God asking me, "Do you *trust* Me? Do you *really trust* Me?" As the Lord tugged at my heart I wrote in my journal:

> *April 5, 2003*
> *Lord, I think I have been bargaining with You my whole life. I think deep down I feel I will do Your work and serve You as long as You protect me and my family. I know that my "happiness" is my stronghold. I can say I trust You or write I trust You, but I am so afraid of what may happen if You remove the "happiness" from my life or my husband's life or my children's lives. How would my trust in You measure up if my faith were put to the test? I want to trust You with every area of my life, my relationship with You, my marriage, my children, and my health. Lord, I am ready for You to work in me and I want to give it all to You. I love You, Lord, and no matter what You do in my life I will still love You even if it doesn't match up with my will. I say this honestly. I turn my will over to You and trust that You will use me so that Your will will shine through so that You may be fully glorified through my life. Whatever that looks like, I am ready for it.*

But I really wasn't. Ten months later, I was driving home from church and felt like I had to get home fast because I needed to go to the bathroom. I pulled into the driveway and ran as fast as I could up to the restroom. I felt severe burning when I urinated. It felt like pain associated with a horrible urinary tract infection, but this burning was worse than I had ever felt before. I kept feeling like I had to go to the bathroom, but after awhile there was nothing left to eliminate; yet the burning remained. I tried to get up from the toilet but every time I tried to stand, pain overwhelmed me. I couldn't even get to a standing position.

I felt so much cramping around my bladder and down in my pelvic area. I just sat there in agony for the next eight hours.

Thankfully, my husband was home to care for the children. He eventually called his mom to come over to help while he sat with me. He kept trying to convince me to let him take me in to the emergency room, but I kept refusing. I insisted that I could not go to the ER for a bladder infection, but I did allow him to call the on-call doctor at our physician's office. I needed some kind of relief. She prescribed an antibiotic that they typically give for urinary tract infections because that is what I told her I thought I had, but it was not helpful. By the next morning, I was feeling a bit better, but I still had lots of cramping and pressure. A little over a week later I felt the same burning feeling when I went to the bathroom and then immediate cramping. This time I called and went in to see the doctor the same day.

They tested my urine and the doctor said, "Good news, you do not have an infection. Just go home, increase your fluids, and you'll be fine." So, I began to drink lots of water, up to eight glasses a day. Two weeks later, I had the pain and burning again and went back to the doctor. Once again, he said, "Good news, you do not have a urinary tract infection. Go home and increase your fluids." But a month later, I was in the doctor's office again. By the end of April, I had been in to see him five times.

I was told to bring in a urine sample and they would test it while I waited in the office. The nurse came out and said, "Good news, you do not have a UTI. Go home and increase your fluids." I broke down in the waiting room and completely lost it. I looked at her and said, "This is not good news. Something is really wrong with me. I have come in for the same thing five times in the last three months. I have increased my fluids to ten glasses of water a day and I am still hurting unbelievably." I told her that I have two young children that I was unable to take care of and I did not feel like myself. She escorted me out of the waiting room and into one of the examining rooms where I waited for my doctor. After repeating the same thing I had just said to the nurse, he suggested that I see a urologist.

In June of that year, 2004, I was diagnosed with a condition called Interstitial Cystitis (IC) and a pelvic floor muscle dysfunction called Levator Ani Syndrome. A test showed that the lining of my bladder wall was cracked and bleeding. Some foods highly irritated my condition. The muscle around the bladder was affected as well, depending on my activity and the extent of damage done inside the bladder wall. My Levator Ani muscle, which runs the entire length of the pelvic floor, was significantly weakened which also caused a significant amount of my pain.

I really didn't know what to think about all of this. I didn't know what either of these conditions really was. I wanted to race home to do research. What effect would these conditions have on my life? I wanted to read about treatments, and about other people with similar experiences. I wanted any kind of information I could get my hands on. I was actually relieved not to hear the big *C* word since they had tested me for cancer as well.

As soon as I received the diagnosis, I wondered, *Could I have done this to myself? Could this be the result of the years of abuse I had put my body through? Poor nutrition? The massive amounts of laxatives I had ingested over the years?* Before I knew it, I blurted out, "Does this have anything to do with poor nutrition or not enough of the right nutrients?" I explained my past history to the urologist and he said it was not likely, but there really is no known cause. As he continued to tell me about these conditions, I almost tuned him out. My preoccupation with the cause was overwhelming. I wondered if my history of laxative abuse had anything to do with my weakened Levator Ani muscle and the history of poor nutrition had anything to do with the lack of protein in the lining of my bladder wall. I have been told repeatedly that there is no evidence of a direct connection between eating disorders and the cause of my health issues, but because there is no known cause, I still continue to wonder.

I was given a list of foods that might be problematic and irritating to my bladder. I was already aware that overdoing it with my activities would cause me pain. I was told that while there is no known cause for these ailments, there is also no known cure for either of these conditions. No cure? I thought, *You mean I will be like this for the rest of my life?*

There were, however, treatments for the symptoms that could put my body into a temporary remission. There were different oral medications that I could take, pain medications, and bladder catheter instillations. For those I needed to come into the office once a week for eight weeks. They would insert a catheter into my urethra and pour the medicine directly into my bladder. I could also try physical therapy and bladder hydro distention surgeries.

The urologist looked at me and said, "So, which one would you like to do?" I thought, *That's it? I have to make up my mind right now?* I was having a hard time internalizing all that he had just said to me. I was still stuck on the fact that this was for *the rest of my life.* At that moment I knew my life was forever changed. *Slam!* I was blind-sided by this blow of health problems. I didn't know what to think or how to feel. I definitely did not feel like the same Leigh-Ann I was just six months before. In fact, I felt like I had lost a big part of who I was and what was familiar. My body wasn't working right and I was less of the wife, mother, and youth leader I wanted to be. Todd wrote in his journal:

> *June 20, 2004*
> *I feel a great sense of relief that Leigh-Ann has some answers for her health issues and that they are not life-threatening. It was difficult to wonder if it was cancer or something like that. I feel sad that our life isn't going to be the same ever again and that for Leigh-Ann it means*

a lifetime of pain and limitations. God, I know there is some reason You are allowing this, but it is painful to watch everything that she is going through. Please deliver her of this. Heal her. Help me to be there to support her anyway I can.

I looked at the restricted food list that was given to me and honestly wondered what I would be able to eat. It listed any foods that contained chocolate, caffeine, carbonation, alcohol, tomatoes, citric acid, and a vast array of spices. I also could not eat fruits other than melons and blueberries, and I could have no Asian, Italian, or Mexican foods. Also on the list was mayonnaise, salad dressing, pepper, marinades, aged cheeses, many different types of dairy products, ketchup, and nothing to drink except milk, water, or decaffeinated tea. It seemed so restrictive. But I went home and changed my diet drastically.

Everything in my life was affected by this pain; the way I played, interacted, and showed affection to my children, my ministry with the senior high girls, my ability to carry out daily responsibilities at home, and even intimacy with my husband.

Everything seemed to hurt. I was thirty-one, much too young to be feeling like this. My body and brain were obviously not on the same page. Inside I felt like I was still twenty, and wanted to be, but I was trapped in this body that did not want to cooperate. I continued to journal and wrote:

July 7, 2004
Dear Heavenly Father, I hurt so much today. I hurt every day. Today my emotions came to a head. I don't know how to feel. I shouldn't be angry, but I am. I don't understand. I can't fix my body, Lord, only You can. I am far from You, but again You have stayed close by me. I sometimes feel You drawing me back to You, but I turn and run the other way. I am so scared.

It has been one month since I was diagnosed with IC. For two weeks now, I have been trying to decide what treatment to go with. I don't like any of the options. They all sound so awful. I don't feel like me anymore. Lord, why must there be so many stumbling blocks along the way? Can't You raise me up another way? My life is so out of control and I can't stand it!

I didn't understand God's purpose. These health issues were certainly not my will and I wasn't sure why it was His. I couldn't comprehend why He would allow me to feel such pain and make it so difficult for me to fulfill the roles He had called me to as a wife, mother, and youth leader. Again I heard his voice, "Leigh-Ann, Do you *trust* Me? Do you *really trust* Me?"

I was fueled by the feelings of my circumstance. All I saw was what I couldn't do, the limitations I had, and how awful the pain was to bear. Honestly, I was scared of what the future held and to have to live like this for the rest of my life. I didn't know how to do that. Todd wrote:

July 15, 2004
God, I am confused with Leigh-Ann's anger and fear. I never think to get angry with You. My first reaction is to get on my knees and pray that the situation will get better. I am definitely sad, but not mad. I know that You are sovereign and good, and You have a plan. I want You to make her better. I am frustrated and I want to know why. I want You to change this, but I am not angry. I know there has to be some reason because I know You don't allow pain or hurt without a purpose. I have to trust in that reason even though I don't have the knowledge of why.

I started to run from God. I could hear Him calling me back, trying to woo me back to Him and tell me truths about who

He is, but I just kept running. His voice was strong, but my determination to run away was stronger. The more I ran from Him, the harder it was to hear His voice. I stopped picking up my Bible, I stopped praying, and I found it hard to journal any feelings but anger, fear, and sadness. I was angry with God that He would allow this in my life, angry with the fact that my life was different, and angry with others who did not know how to respond compassionately.

I felt like I didn't know how to relate to the people in my life any longer and they didn't know how to relate to me. Emily and Christopher, then six and three, had to deal with *Mommy can't do this or that* and it just seemed so unfair for them since they were really too young to understand. They began to worry about what was wrong with me and started to become afraid of why I wasn't like I used to be.

Our friends started to see changes in who I was and in how I related to them. I pulled away from them all, shut them out, and closed into myself emotionally. My relationships became superficial and I wasn't sure how to act around my friends. I wanted them to think that I could deal with all that was going on in my life, without these conditions changing my life. I wanted them to think I could handle the pain and still do the same things or be the same person I was before. I wanted to be able to handle it all. I didn't want to alienate my friends by dwelling on my pain, so I never spoke of it. I didn't want to be the wet blanket on all the fun, so I tried my best to hide how I was feeling, emotionally and physically.

I heard a whole realm of reactions and opinions from well-meaning, all-knowing people with good intentions. Some felt sorry for me and treated me as if I were a child or damaged goods and could not talk about *my problem* in front of me. Or they would say that I could no longer do things for myself. Others judged and questioned how bad my pain really was if they couldn't tell I was hurting. What they didn't know was that one day of hiding my pain and pretending I was fine, by doing things I shouldn't do, could cause me pain for the next three days. Carrying too much, joining in an activity that was too physically stressful, overdoing it with commitments and not resting, or eating something I shouldn't so I wouldn't hurt someone's feelings, led to extreme physical consequences. I didn't want to hurt, but I was also terrified to let anyone know that I was hurting or that my life had even changed at all.

Yet others, who were well-meaning but totally misguided, tried to tell me not to be angry with God. Since I was a strong woman, they knew I could get through this. They would say I needed to just have faith, or a stronger faith, and then He would heal me, and in the end what a great testimony I would have. Those words made me angry. I think this response upset me the most. Oh, how their good intentions and inspiring words had really become so hurtful.

I never doubted God could heal me, but I wasn't sure that He would. I knew that there was no guarantee of that, or that His plan to do so was dependent upon how much faith I had or how hard I prayed. I wasn't sure if that was in His plan for me and I certainly did not feel strong. I felt weak and broken. I was hurt by the words that God could use me greatly if He healed me and what great testimonies people have because the Lord has healed them. I was happy for those who had experienced healing or changed circumstances, but a part of me would get angry to hear those testimonies.

I thought, *What about the person God chooses not to heal? The one who continues to live in pain? The one who doesn't get to have the happily ever after? The one who still has to live with a loss? What about them? Where is God in all of that?* What got me into trouble in the first place was buying into the Christian view that the life we live is a constant fairy tale, and if we face a difficulty, then all we have to do is trust that God will remove it from our lives. I wanted just one person to be real with me and stop pretending that even if they were handed the worst news possible, they would be okay with it. I was angry and scared, and I didn't know what to do with all of that.

I would also hear reactions like, "Well, at least you don't have cancer. It's not like you are going to die from this." And that was right. This was not a life-threatening illness and the treatments were not like chemotherapy. I thanked God every day for that, but I did have to live with this for the rest of my life—unless He chose to heal me. I needed to learn how I was going to do that in so much pain and come to an acceptance and reconciliation with Him. I had thought those same thoughts and felt guilty for feeling the way I did when I knew there were others out there going through much more difficult circumstances than I was. But that reaction from others still hurt tremendously.

I tried as hard as I could to pretend as if everything was okay. I never let anyone see me hurt. I hid it well and continued with life as if nothing had changed. I painted on the plastic smile, terrified to show how I was really feeling. I was a pro at hiding my feelings and my pain. It was really less about pride and more about fear of the reactions from others—rejection, judgment, or pity that might be lurking just around the corner to cause me more pain.

If anyone asked how I was doing, I would turn on the upbeat tone and say the familiar, "fine," "good," or "doing well, thanks for asking." If I could hide from all these people, then maybe, just maybe, I would really start to believe that I *was* fine, good, and doing well. In reality, however, I was not. In truth, I was hurting in a way that I had never hurt before. I was more scared than I ever had been and more angry than I care to admit.

Treading on Familiar Territory

After I had been told about the food irritants, I immediately developed a fear of food. If I ate the wrong thing, I would hurt, and it burned. I hated the burning feeling. I could tolerate the muscle pain much more, even though it sometimes affected my walking. The doctor had said, "You just have to figure out by trial and error what you can eat on this list ." Honestly, I didn't want to find out. I was afraid to hurt. I took it upon myself to restrict everything on the list. My anger and fear seemed to manifest again in wanting to control my life. Soon I noticed that, more and more, I was beginning to restrict foods that were okay to eat. I started fearing them, too. I became obsessive about what went into my mouth until I really wasn't consuming much of anything. My eating disorder had again reared its ugly head.

As I was getting dressed one morning, Todd asked me if I was doing okay with eating because I had become so thin. He journaled:

July 26, 2004
I can tell Leigh-Ann is losing weight. I think it is mostly because of the IC. I know she is unable to eat like she used to because of it. I am not sure that is the only reason. I think she is struggling with eating. I don't know what to do. I don't want to accuse her of something that she may not be doing and make her angry and offended, but I am also afraid that something is just not right. I can't put my finger on it. I can't make her eat.

I told Todd that I was struggling, a little, but that I was still in complete control. I journaled:

July 26, 2004
I know Todd is worried and feels completely out of control, but what is so ironic is that, over the same issue, I feel completely in control. I am really thriving on that. It feels comfortable and secure. I am holding on tight to the notion that I am in control of at least one thing. It has been two weeks of bladder instillations and one week of medications. My hair is extremely dry, but so

79

far no loss. I keep waiting for the instillations to kick in. I am in such a hard place right now—in the midst of treatments and still feeling like crap. I am so bitter. Lord, every day I know that You are calling to me. I keep running. My mind races with conflicting thoughts: eat, don't eat; be angry, don't be angry; run away, don't run away. I don't know where I am spiritually. I feel like I am one of the large engine trains in the story The Little Engine That Could. The ones that refuse to pull the long train of freight cars up the mountain because it was too much pull for them. I want to be able to strap on the freight cars and believe You when I hear You say, "I know you can, I know you can." Instead, I get scared and choose to stay where I know it's safe, down at the bottom of the mountain looking up at what seems completely impossible. It's getting easier to restrict and harder and harder to eat. I feel that fear of food getting more intense. I have lost any appetite I did have. I am starting down that black hole again. Please, Lord, don't let me hit bottom.

Journal Questions

1. What are you running from, angry about, or afraid of?

2. Have you become weak and broken? If so, in what ways?

3. What circumstances in your life are you expecting God to heal or change?

4. What are you bound and determined not to let anyone see?

5. Are there conflicting thoughts in your head? If so, what are they?

Prayer

Dear Heavenly Father,
I am weak and broken. I am living a life away from You. Help me to see that You are in complete control of what makes me scared or causes me pain. Help me to trust in You. Amen.

CHAPTER 8

Rock Bottom... or So I Thought

*In your anger do not sin. Do not let the sun go down
while you are still angry, and do not give the devil a foothold.*
Ephesians 4:26-27

I was a good patient, doing the things I was told, restricting foods, going through treatments, and taking medications. But, nothing seemed to help and I was becoming more frustrated and angry.

I was so confused. My feelings were all so real and now, once again, my eating had become out of control. My good friend Susie, who was also my pastor's wife, noticed how thin I had become and confronted me about my eating. I told her I was struggling, and she pleaded with me to give it over to God. I told her I was not ready to do that. I found comfort in not eating. It gave me security to be in control of my weight. She said, "So, how is that working for you? The way I see it, so far, not eating has only taken you further from God and your husband. You're hurting your kids, jeopardizing your ministry, and you still feel angry."

Susie was the one person who said, "It's okay to be angry. It does stink what you are going through. I'm sorry you have to go through it, but you have to work through your anger with God. Battle it out with Him. Otherwise, you will remain stuck in the anger and fear, and continue to run from Him."

She reminded me that God knew what I was going through. It was part of His plan, even if I didn't like it. He already knew how I was feeling, so why try to hide from Him?

Battling it out with God was such a hard concept for me. How do you *battle it out* with the Holy One? What about reverence, respect, and a fear of the Lord? I was having a hard time facing the fact that I was so angry, even though I knew I was. The entire time I was running from God, angry at Him, and fueled by my fear, I felt like I was being irreverent. I felt that if this was His plan and will for my life, then I should just accept it and move on. Who was I to question God, anyway? However, I could not just accept it and move on. There was a huge emotional battle going on inside of me about how I thought I should be feeling and the way I *really* was feeling.

Susie suggested that I go away for a time to sit at God's feet, maybe to a hotel or somewhere by myself for a night, with no distractions. Talk to Him, plead with Him, cry, yell, whatever it would take to work through my feelings with the Lord, which I knew I needed to do. I couldn't keep living like this, but I was terrified. I felt paralyzed to leave her house that day. I walked out to my car, but couldn't get in. Leaving meant I had to face my fears, face God, and confront my anger.

Todd agreed that I needed to have some solitude with God and supported my decision to go. So, I made plans to go to a nice hotel that weekend while he would be off work to care for the children. When Friday afternoon came, I was hesitant to go, but I knew that I needed to. This was not going to be a time of respite and relaxation. I knew that facing this pain was not going to be easy.

After much urging from Todd, I kissed him goodbye, got into my car, and drove to the hotel. When I got to the parking lot, my apprehension to go in was overwhelming. I sat in my car for over an hour and considered going home. Just what was I supposed to say? How was this going to work? By the time I mustered up the courage to go in and up to my room, I was in so much pain that I could barely stand. I don't know if it was the stress or anticipation, but whatever the reason, I was hurting terribly. As soon as I entered the room, I got into the shower for some relief. Since I still couldn't stand up, I crouched down and let the water hit my back. I began to cry. Initially my tears were because the pain was so great, but as I began to pray, they fell because of anger, sadness, and fear.

I asked God the obvious question, "Why?" I was pleading for the Lord to take away my pain. I said lots of things I never expected to say, things I didn't even know I was feeling. The pain grew in intensity.

I got out of the shower and looked at the clock. I had been in the shower for two hours. It was strange. I had no concept that much time had passed. The water never got cold and I never ran out of words to say or tears to cry. I got dressed and laid down on the bed, still in terrible agony. I felt exhausted already, but I knew I was nowhere near finished. I had spewed out all my feelings, but had not come to a hope, trust, or reconciliation with my God. I didn't know where to go from there, so I just opened my Bible to Psalm 25. Todd told me to read it while I was gone. It was right on the money.

> To you, O Lord, I lift up my soul; in you I trust, O
> my God. ... No one whose hope is in you will ever be
> put to shame ... Show me your ways, O Lord, teach me
> your paths; guide me in your truth ... or you are God, my
> Savior, and my hope is in you all day long. Remember,
> O Lord, your great mercy and love ... for you are good
> ... Good and upright is the Lord;... All the ways of the
> Lord are loving and faithful ... My eyes are ever on the
> Lord, for only he will release my feet from the snare.
> Turn to me and be gracious to me, for I am lonely and
> afflicted. The troubles of my heart have multiplied;
> free me from my anguish. Look upon my affliction and
> distress ... Guard my life and rescue me;... for I take

85

refuge in you. May integrity and uprightness protect me,
because my hope is in you.

I was shocked by the words I was reading. I don't know why. I know that God's Word is living and active, but I was truly amazed at its significance in my life at that very moment. In the shower, I had cried out to God, "I don't trust You. You have hurt me, and I don't understand Your ways. How can You love me and allow me to hurt? Right now, I don't feel like You are good or loving or faithful. I can handle this on my own and I will not take refuge in You."

The Psalmist said, "I trust in you, hope in you, show me your ways, The Lord is good and all his ways are loving and faithful, only He will release my feet from the snare for I will take refuge in you."

Wow, those words spoke right to the heart of it all. I cried out, "Take it away; I don't want to hurt anymore," but He didn't take it away. I yelled at Him, "I don't believe that You promise to never give someone more than they can handle because I wake up in pain every morning. Sometimes I find it difficult to even get to the bathroom, and I face my pain all day long. I'm not able to take care of my children, and I go to bed in pain, only to wonder what tomorrow's pain will be like. This is more than I can handle. I can't live like this and I don't want to live like this." I cried out, "What do You want from me?" And then I heard His reply within the words I had just read, "I want you to trust Me and take refuge in Me. Do you *trust* Me, Leigh-Ann? Do you *really trust* Me?"

That night in the hotel room, I tried to work through my anger with God. At one point, I really thought I wasn't angry with Him anymore. I thought I had accepted that there was a purpose for this. But truthfully, I had only accepted it with the notion that I could live with pain and that my physical life would be difficult, as long as I would have moments of normal life when the treatments began to work and the medication kicked in.

I was trying to bargain with God. Not everything that I knew in my head was translating into what I felt in my heart. I realized that this had become the pattern of my spiritual life. I had lots of head knowledge of the right things to say, but when my faith was put to the test, my acceptance was conditional. I thought I could handle it if I could have some of my life back every once in awhile. But weeks later, it was still apparent that I was angry. Todd wrote:

> *August 27, 2004*
> *I went in to see Pastor Paul. He wanted to talk about me about how I was doing, but I didn't want to talk about it. I feel pretty numb at this point. I wanted to talk about Leigh-Ann and how to help her. I just want her to be better. She is angry and struggling. She went to a hotel to work out her anger with God. I hoped that whatever transpired there would make her better. I wanted to believe it helped, but it didn't change anything. She is still angry.*

A few weeks later I wrote in my journal.

> *September 15, 2004*
> *It is 2 A.M. I woke up out of a dead sleep by a terrible pain in my bladder area. I had to pee, but that only worsened my pain. I crawled back to bed. I had my last bladder instillation yesterday. It was awful. It is always awful. The latex-free catheters are not as pliable as the regular ones, so they hurt so much more. They stiffen and don't allow the medicine to flow easily into my bladder. The pressure pushes the catheter out and the medicine always ends up all over me. Most days we repeat the process over and over until the medicine is successfully*

inside, which means reinserting the catheter two or three times in an already painful area. Today the nurse was moving it all around to see if she could keep it in. It hurt so much I thought I was going to be sick. Tears welled up in my eyes and trickled down the side of my face into my ear. I closed my eyes and thought of our vacations on the beach. When the nurse finished she asked me how I had been feeling. That was my last instillation of the series and I had not felt any better. They hurt so much. I could not take it any longer. I told her not to worry about it, but that I would not be back. I got to the car and cried in the parking lot of the doctors' office. Eight weeks of catheter hell and I still don't feel any better. In my mind I keep thinking I can handle the rough times and just really live in those times of remission. Now I see the bitter reality; remission may never come. My life will never be the same. The hope of those glimpses of normalcy is gone. There is nothing left to do.

That day I struggled in the car to find hope. I was frustrated and really angry. I didn't know how to be okay with this. No normalcy, no remission, no glimpses of how I used to live my life. I wanted to know why and I demanded that the Lord give me an explanation if He wasn't going to heal me. Why couldn't He just give me moments of remission? How was I supposed to live every day like this? I didn't know how to accept it now. And, yes, more anger.

I felt ashamed and angry that I was angry. I felt just as confused as ever and continued to hold onto the control and security I had with my eating. In my head, I wanted to trust God. I wanted to believe that this was part of His perfect plan for me, but clearly I was not okay with it all and held ever so tightly to my false security. I continued with the same journal entry:

I know I should give this anorexia over to You, but I don't want to. I am not giving You that, too. I know it is a crutch, I know it is unhealthy. I know it could destroy me. I know, I know, I know, but no! I had accepted that life would be difficult until remission comes, but remission didn't come. Why not? I don't understand! Now I am feeling more angry than ever and hurt and in pain. Why am I up at 2 a.m. feeling pain? Why is it that the last thing I am aware of at night before I close my eyes is pain and the first thing I am aware of in the morning when I open my eyes is pain?

My friend Mary sent me a card today and it said Exodus 15:26: "I am the Lord who heals you." I got an email from my friend Jenn today. She said that as she was praying, the Lord directed her to pray for healing for me and that she was reminded of the story from Luke 8:40, how Jesus healed the bleeding woman just as she touched His robe. My friend said, "I am going to pray for healing." As I was tucking Emily into bed, she asked me, "Why won't God heal you so you won't hurt and we can have fun again?" Yes, God, if You are a God who heals, why won't You heal me so that I can have fun again, live again, and be me again? I hate this and I don't understand why it is part of Your plan.

Todd recognized that I was still struggling with my eating and he urged me to begin counseling. He continued to journal:

September 18, 2004
Something has to give. Leigh-Ann keeps getting skinnier and skinnier. I don't know what to do or how to help. I think she is still under the illusion that it is because of the IC or that she is in complete control, but

*I know it's more than that, more than she can handle
on her own.*

A friend of mine from church was a Christian counselor and
worked with women who had eating disorders. She is very wise,
grounded in her faith and I trusted her. I knew things weren't
getting better, so I called and made an appointment to meet with
her. During the first few sessions we caught up with what had
been happening in my life over the last several months. Then
one evening our session really hit a nerve. She asked me how I
was handling day-to-day life with my IC. I said, "I am having
a hard time being okay with everything. It doesn't feel okay
to not be physical with the kids. It doesn't feel okay to not be
able to be physical with my husband. I don't feel like a whole
person and that is not okay." I shared my frustration in trying
to work it out with God and still coming up feeling angry.

She asked me if I had grieved. I responded that was what I
did in the hotel room. She said, "No, you yelled and screamed
and expressed your anger. You tried to make a deal with God,
and the acceptance you came to was conditional; but have you
grieved?" She continued, "There is a toughness about you,
Leigh-Ann. I have not seen you grieve. I have not heard you
talk about grieving the loss of the life you once had."

She told me that acceptance will come, and my anger will
only subside once I have grieved. I laughed and told her I was
not going to do that. She said, "There it is. You are running,
shutting down, putting up that tough exterior, yet inside you
are angry, crying, and taking it all out on yourself." She said,
"I suspect you have always handled your pain this way. It is
easier for you to shut down, numb out, and put up that brick
wall than it is for you to be honest about how you are truly
feeling." She was completely right, and I hated that. I hated
that she knew how I was feeling. She knew I was angry and
ashamed, and dying inside.

She quoted Hosea 7:14: "They do not cry out to me from their hearts but wail upon their beds. They gather together for grain and new wine but turn away from me." She ended our time by reminding me that when I feel angry and ashamed, the Lord wants me to cry out to Him and seek refuge in Him. She said there is a difference between grieving, being honest with my feelings, and wallowing in self-pity. I wrote in my journal again:

> *October, 3, 2004*
> *Well, Lord, here I am struggling more than ever. I am desperately holding on to the anorexia. My thoughts and actions have become obsessive. I am not giving it over to You. I am not sure why I find so much comfort in something that is so desperately dangerous. Why is it that this has become more important to me than You? I saw myself in the mirror naked, and it both scared me and made me feel victorious. I weigh less than I ever have since junior high school. I am obsessed with the numbers again. I am weighing myself several times a day, and Todd has no idea I even have a scale.*

Each Sunday morning I could tell I was running farther and farther away. My worship became less heartfelt until I stopped singing altogether. I had become more distracted and less focused during the message, until I no longer made eye contact with the pastor and refused to look at the Cross hanging in the sanctuary. At the same time, the Holy Spirit churned up so much inside of me.

By now I had been working with the youth of our church for three years. I was now co-leading my group with a good friend of mine, so that if there were times I needed to miss because of my pain, she could cover for me. One Sunday evening at youth group, the worship team began to sing. I was feeling a lot of pain that day, so I could not stand for the entire time.

91

My pain was great, but I was also so weak. I had lost a total of fifty-five pounds at that point and was still not eating.

Even though I felt so far from God, the words of the songs began to touch me. I was convicted of my sin. My pain continued to increase and tears welled up in my eyes. I tried to fight them back, but they just would not stop. I made my way out of the youth room and into the empty sanctuary. I saw the Cross and went to my knees. The tears kept coming. I didn't know what to do or what to say. I could feel the Lord drawing me back, but I was so deep into controlling my food once again. Here I was thinking all along that I was the one in control, when really the eating disorder had control over me.

How had I let it get that far? When did it happen? I wanted God to light His fire in my heart again, but my flesh was so weak. I was reminded of Romans 7:15-25:

> *I do not understand what I do. For what I want to do I do not do, but what I hate I do. And if I do what I do not want to do, I agree that the law is good. As it is, it is no longer I myself who do it, but it is sin living in me. I know that nothing good lives in me, that is, in my sinful nature. For I have the desire to do what is good, but I cannot carry it out. For what I do is not the good I want to do; no, the evil I do not want to do—this I keep on doing. Now if I do what I do not want to do, it is no longer I who do it, but it is sin living in me that does it. So I find this law at work: When I want to do good, evil is right there with me. For in my inner being I delight in God's law; but I see another law at work in the members of my body, waging war against the law of my mind and making me a prisoner of the law of sin at work within my members. What a wretched man I am! Who will rescue me from this body of death? Thanks be to God—through Jesus Christ our Lord! So then, I*

myself in my mind am a slave to God's law, but in the
sinful nature a slave to the law of sin.

My time at the Cross truly brought my sin to light. I felt convicted as I thought about Christ's sacrifice for me and my selfishness about remaining in control. I recognized my sin was not just about what I was doing to my body, but also it was about my conditionally trusting God with my entire life. It was about hanging on to my comfort and my control, instead of allowing Him to work in my life. I felt ashamed, but I was still unwilling to take action and give it all up.

I continued that downward spiral again, adding vomiting to my array of ways to control my weight. I only ate when I had to, and then I vomited it up. I vomited before and after my counseling sessions. It became aggressive. I knew I definitely had a problem and didn't know how to solve it; and I was not sure I wanted to. In a strange way, there was comfort in the control I thought I had, but at the same time there was an underlying fear of where this was all heading.

Susie confronted me again. She said she had been thinking about me and praying for me for three days and that her husband, my pastor, had noticed me in church and knew that I was not doing well. He asked if they needed to take me to the hospital. She said people at church were asking her if I was okay.

I shared a little of how I was feeling and even less about what I was doing. She actually gave me no choice. It had become difficult to cover up the wasting away of my body. She said I needed to wrestle with God again because the first time my acceptance had been conditional. I told her I knew that in my heart, but I wasn't ready to give the anorexia over to Him. As irrational as that was, it had become my complete comfort and was at the same time slowly taking my life.

She said, "Leigh-Ann, you don't have much time. You are wasting away to nothing. This is killing you." Stubbornly, I responded, "Nothing physical has happened to me yet. When it gets that far, I will stop." She said, "I don't think you can stop until you face God and let Him work in you." At that point, that was something I was not willing to do. I was bitter, angry, running scared, and clearly a slave to the sin.

That night I had a counseling session. I vomited before I went in. Before we started, my counselor said, "I have been thinking about you and praying for you for three days." She confronted me with some of the same things Susie had. It was a difficult session. She asked me, "What hold does this disorder have on you? Why is it so important to you and why has it become more important than your health, your husband, your children, and your relationship with God?"

Good questions. I wanted to know, too. There was a cancellation for the hour right after mine. My counselor asked me if I wanted to stay. I did. I was still feeling the effects of vomiting. I was extremely upset from what we had been discussing and having a hard time focusing on what she was saying. I felt sick. I told her I needed to go to the bathroom. As I stood up, I passed out. It seemed my body always reacted the same way when I abused it.

Once I came to, I begged her not to call the paramedics and not to ask me to go to the hospital. Instead, she asked me to have someone pick me up and drive me home. I couldn't believe that God had laid me on the hearts of these two wise women, who felt for three days to be on their knees for me, not knowing why. I called some friends to pick me up and take me home.

On the way home, I kept saying how terrified I was and that I never intended to let it get that bad. I had said I would stop before anything physical happened. But now I was totally consumed by the disorder and in complete denial of the possibility that something serious was happening as a result of abusing my body.

When had it taken control again? At some point I had lost the control. The comfort became desperation and I didn't even realize when it had happened. I was terrified of what might happen next. When I got home, I had to face Todd and tell him what happened. That was difficult for me. I didn't want to hurt him anymore than I already had. He wrote:

> *October, 14, 2004*
> *I am worried and scared about what is happening to Leigh-Ann. Why is she afraid to talk to me? Why did she call friends to bring her home? Why didn't she call me? She said she didn't want to tell me on the phone. She didn't want me to be thinking about it all the way to pick her up. She wanted to talk to me face to face, but I feel so stupid. I should have seen that she was getting worse.*

Journal Questions

1. Read Romans 7:15-25. What is it that you do that you don't want to do? Who will rescue you from this?

2. How has the *comfort* you have found in food evolved into desperation?

3. Is there something in your life that you need to battle out with God?

3. What is it that you need to first grieve over and then accept in your life?

4. How are you trying to bargain with God or where has your acceptance become conditional?

5. Read Psalm 25. How are these verses speaking to you?

6. What does seeking refuge in Him look like in your life?

Prayer

Dear Heavenly Father,

If there is something in my life that I have given You conditionally or that I am trying to bargain with You, help me to see that I need to battle it out with You until I can come to a changed heart and acceptance of it in my life. Help me to seek You for refuge and strength. Amen.

CHAPTER 9

Answers in My Father's Chair

"My Father's chair sits in a royal room.
My Father's chair holds glory beyond the tomb.
My Father's chair my God is there and I am His eternally.
My Father's chair. My Father's chair."
– David Parkes[1]

Three weeks after the fainting experience in my counselor's office, I found myself headed to a retreat center with six other women. I already knew three of them from church, but the other three were friends of Susie's, whom I had not met. The center was located on 300 acres and nestled in one-hundred-year-old pine trees. It was secluded and we were there to retreat. Susie had planned that we would have some time to get to know each other, but also some time to be in solitude. I found a room to use for my time alone with God. It had a box filled with sand and a kneeling stool. It had a bay window that looked out to the enormous pines. In front of the window was a chair that was the perfect mix of comfortable and firm. It was tall and winged back, and I felt like a little girl sitting in her father's chair. We had three large blocks of time by ourselves. During the first block I wrote in my journal:

November 7, 2004

Lord, help me to use this time wisely at Your feet. Help me to see what You want from this time alone with You. I love You and I want to be close to You again, but I can't. I do not understand Your ways, but I want to. Help me to see why it is so hard for me to trust You, receive comfort from You, and why I get so angry for the things You have allowed in my life. Help me to not be afraid to hurt or to face those difficult issues in my life, but to find my strength in You.

I spent much of that time frustrated, angry, and again asking God, *Why so much pain?* I began to truly recognize and understand that my obsession with food and weight was how I dealt all along with the pain and hurt in my life.

The second time of solitude I spent grieving. The tears just came and I could not get them to stop. I thought about what my counselor had said about my toughness. Now it was gone. I thought about the life I was leaving, the life of physical strength and a pain-free body, and I wept. Finally, I could truly grieve. I was crying so much I could barely keep up with my thoughts. The pages of my journal were soaked, and the ink began to run and bleed through. I was scared, angry, repentant, and at His feet. I thought about the woman who had washed Jesus' feet with her tears and in that moment I felt like I was doing the same.

During the third time of solitude I walked into my quiet room and crawled up into "my Father's chair." I was physically hurting and could not get a handle on my pain, so I curled up and was still. Quietly I sat, with a heart receptive to God's revelations. I had a strong sense that He was not going to heal me; that I would always face this pain. Again I questioned, "Why the pain, Lord, and must it be lifelong? Can't You take it away at some point?" I was still stuck in the hope that He would heal me, deliver me, and rescue me from this pain. I didn't want to be angry anymore, but waiting for the rescue that just didn't happen kept me feeling like God had let me down, walked away, or turned a blind eye to my distress.

After much prayer, I realized that maybe it wasn't part of God's plan to heal me physically. Maybe He had purpose for this pain. I knew that no amount of prayer or how deeply I believed would take away my pain until God was finished using it in my life. However, prayer is powerful. I needed to remain on my knees because even though my prayers wouldn't change God's mind, they were changing my heart. They might not alter His plan, but they would fulfill it, and while they were not going to bend God's will to mine, they would align my will with His. And again God said, "Leigh-Ann, do you *trust* Me? Do you *really trust* Me?"

I realized that my faith should not be based on healing, but rather on God's plan for me. I thought back to the day I received the card with Exodus 15:26: "I am the Lord who heals," the email from my friend who was so sure I would be healed, and Emily's asking me why the Lord wouldn't heal me. That was a difficult day. And then there it was. God spoke, not audibly but in my heart: "My healing for you, Leigh-Ann, is not of the physical kind, but of the spiritual kind. I *am* a Lord who heals and I did reveal to your friend through prayer that you would be healed. When you have grown, Emily will see that. I am restoring your soul and preparing you for what I have in store."

I thought of Christ's words to Peter in John 13:7: "You do not realize now what I am doing, but later you will understand." I walked over to the sand box, knelt, and wrote the words: "Joy," "Love," "Faith," "Forgiveness," "Grace," and "Peace."

Then I went back and sat comfortably in "my Father's chair," looking out over the pines. It was so quiet, so peaceful. I didn't want to leave. I yearned for more of that solitude with God.

In between our times of solitude, we women talked about our lives, our times of struggle, pain, and hardship, and about our growth in Christ. This was overwhelmingly difficult for me since I was currently in the eye of one of those times. The love and support from the other women was incredible, even from those I had just met. Our hearts were forever knitted together that weekend, and lasting Christ-centered friendships were formed.

I realized during this retreat that the answers to all of my questions hinged on my ability to trust in God's plan. Little by little, He was revealing more of that to me. Now I knew the truth, but I would still need to understand how to live that truth out in my life.

Journal Questions

1. What about prayer do you know to be true?

2. What is true about the Lord's healing power?

3. What truth do you know in your head, but still haven't been able to live out in your life?

Prayer

Dear Heavenly Father,
Help me to understand the purpose of my prayers and look at the motivations of what I ask. Help me, Lord, to understand that Your healing power is much more than just physical; it is spiritual as well. Help me to live out what I know is true. Amen.

CHAPTER 10

No More Sifting

*Simon, Simon, Satan has asked to sift you as wheat. But I have
prayed for you, Simon, that your faith may not fail. And when you
have turned back, strengthen your brothers.*
Luke 22:31-32

Not even three weeks after I returned home from the retreat,
we started to see nervous and disruptive behaviors in our
six-year-old daughter. She was biting her fingernails, clinging
to me, throwing up randomly, and was, seemingly, stressed out.
She had even displayed disruptive behavior at school. We knew
we were facing some difficult issues in her life.

I became more and more concerned and preoccupied with
what was going on in that little head of hers. I started to feel
sad and extremely guilty that I may have been so wrapped up
in my own difficulties that I missed what was going on with
her. I journaled my feelings and prayed for wisdom. I asked the
Lord to help me to trust Him with this. Now it was no longer
about my life; it was about hers.

I was watching my little girl change from happy and carefree
to worried and stressed out. I didn't know how to help her
or what to do. I thought as Christmas approached, with all
the fun and excitement that accompanies it, surely she will be
back to normal. Christmas came and went and there was no
change. Emily still seemed so unlike herself. I felt guilty and

responsible. I kept thinking, *What did I miss and why can't I fix this? Slam!* Blind-sided again, but this time by the blow of reality that I cannot protect my children from hurt and pain. We live in a fallen world. It is inevitable that we will and our children will face hardships and trials, but she was so young in age and in her faith. I wanted to protect her from harm. I wanted to take away her pain. I am her mother and couldn't stop her hurting. God said, "Leigh-Ann, do you *trust* Me? Do you *really trust* Me?"

Subconsciously, I started to become even more aggressive with my eating disorder. For four weeks, nothing stayed in my system. The intensity of restricting food and vomiting felt violent and harmful, different from how it had ever felt in the past. I think I was doing it now out of a disdain for myself and the guilt I carried for missing what was happening to my little girl. I continued to journal:

> *January 17,2005*
> *I ate nothing all day, but then at 6 p.m. I had half of a plain bagel and two bites of a banana. The feeling to get rid of it was overwhelming. No choice but to. Vomiting hurt so much tonight, but I couldn't stop. I watched until there was nothing left to throw up and then I just kept going. I am not sure why. I knew there was nothing left in my stomach, but I just couldn't stop. My throat hurt terribly, but I didn't care. Uh-oh, I think I am definitely going over the edge. This time feels more intense and more aggressive than it ever has in the past. I have been so very violent with it all. At this rate, I know it won't be long before it affects me physically. I mean, I guess more physically than it has already. Don't want to get there, but my feelings are so intense now. I am not sure how to get out of this pit. A part of me is scared to continue, but a bigger part of me is scared to give it up. There is this constant battle inside of me.*

The turmoil is so great. I hate that I am giving Satan a foothold in my life, but I know it is my choice to not eat and to throw up. I know what this can do to me if I don't fight those irrational thoughts and temptations, but I am exhausted. I am definitely losing this battle. There is not much fight in me anymore.

At this point, I was more deceptive than ever. Todd was still watching me to see how I was doing, so I was very sneaky. I ate nothing for breakfast or lunch. I would eat a small portion at dinner and tell him I was not hungry because I had eaten more at the other two meals. I would volunteer to get the kids ready for bed so I could go away from where he was, to vomit.

After Todd left for work at 11 p.m., I would get on the treadmill and begin to run. I would run and run and run with tears streaming down my face from the pain of the IC and weakened Levator Ani muscle. I refused to stop until I collapsed in pain. I would head back upstairs to vomit some more. A few times after vomiting late into the night, I actually slept on the bathroom floor because it hurt too much to get up, and I was too dizzy anyway to get up to bed. On several occasions, I vomited so much I began to have chest pain and thought I would pass out again. One evening I was so aggressive that it blurred the vision in my right eye. I was clearly punishing myself. I prayed:

Lord, I am so sorry for all of this, but this is my daughter, my child. She is hurting. I don't know all the details of why and I can't fix it. Why was I so wrapped up in my own issues that I missed what was happening in her life? No more sifting! You said You would never give anyone more than they can handle, but I am tired of the sifting, tired of the lessons to be learned. I can't take any more.

But the Lord knew how much I could take. He knew with His strength I could prevail. He knew that His plan was perfect for me and there was much more sifting to do. My life felt like a roller coaster. Even in counseling, I was experiencing a losing battle with this addiction. I felt like I would take one step forward and two steps back anytime the Lord allowed a hardship in my life.

Stand by Me

I had a dream one night that bothered me for days. In my dream, I was running late for church. I hurried around the house getting ready, dressing my best, and perfectly doing my hair and makeup. Once the kids were ready, we all hopped into the car and rushed to church. We came in late, dropped the kids off at their classes, and went into the service, which was already in session. It was full, jammed with people.

There were no seats available. Our pastor was already talking, and Todd and I were wandering around looking for a place to sit. A man looked at Todd and said, "Here is your seat," pointing to one empty chair. Todd sat down and I was left to search for a place to sit. I spotted an empty seat on the other side of the sanctuary. When I made my way over, I saw a woman in the seat next to the empty chair. She was extremely overweight. In fact, she was enormously obese. She was the largest woman I had ever seen. She frightened me. I went to sit down, but she was taking up her seat and most of mine. She knocked me over and I fell to the ground. Each time I tried to get back up and sit in the seat, she knocked me to the floor.

I was so afraid, I wanted to leave. I looked up at our pastor and he said, "Stay, Leigh-Ann. Please stay. You have to stay." But I was shaking in fear. I didn't want to fight the woman anymore. I just wanted to run away. I looked at Susie, who was sitting in the chair in front of me, and she said, "Here, Leigh-Ann, you can have my seat, and I will stand by you."

When I woke up from my dream, I was shaking and tears were streaming down my face. I felt terrified of the obese woman. I thought about that dream repeatedly. It was so symbolic of the fear in my life, the disorder that kept knocking me to the ground, and the loving friend who was willing to "stand by me." Little did I realize just how willing Susie was to stand by me, until a few days later.

One morning, while I was getting dressed, Todd asked me how I was doing. He said he felt far from me. He told me that lately I was so distant and he felt like God was telling him I wasn't doing well. I was nervous about how to respond to Todd. I didn't want to hurt him. I didn't want to lie to him. But if I told him the truth, then I would have to let go of my control, my comfort, and my security.

I couldn't look at him. I gave a little nervous laugh and tried to make him feel bad for even asking. I said, "If you feel far from me, then maybe it's because of you, not me." Now I really felt awful. Not only did I lie to the person I loved and adored the most in the whole world, but I was making him feel guilty for questioning about how I was doing. I never felt so ashamed as I did at that moment. Yet still in the back of my mind, I felt I had no choice. Todd journaled:

January 26, 2005
I am angry and frustrated that Leigh-Ann is lying to me. There are so many lies and so much deception. She says, "I'm fine," then she passes out. She says that scared her and she is doing better now, but I don't know what to believe anymore. I think she is running on the treadmill when she promised me she wouldn't. She has a nervous laugh she does when she is uncomfortable with me asking her how she is doing or when I think she is lying to me. I get so angry at the nervous laugh. I want to yell at her, "Why are you laughing when I am hurting, when I am worried about you and worried

about our marriage? Don't you care?" I feel so far from her and wonder if, and when, she is lying to me? God always gives me a sense of when she isn't being truthful. I feel sick inside.

The next afternoon I had lunch with Susie. I had been anxious about meeting with her for days. I was nervous about what would transpire in our conversation. I didn't know how long I could continue hiding from the people who loved me most. I considered canceling a couple of times, but I had to talk to her about a speaking engagement for the youth girls, and I wondered if she would be asking why I wanted to cancel. I kept our lunch date, but continued to worry. Susie was running a little late. As I waited, I became even more anxious, hoping that maybe she would just not show. She was a little late, but she did come.

During our lunch, I wondered if Susie would notice that I was just picking at my food. I had to eat. But how would I excuse myself to go to the bathroom without her questioning me or following me in? Would she notice that I was still dropping weight? I wore a big sweater hoping she wouldn't notice.

Then she asked, "How are you doing, Leigh-Ann?" I couldn't look at her. Could I lie, again? This was much like my conversation the day before with Todd and many years ago with Kay. How I hated all the lies. These people were so dear to me. They cared about me and I was so deceitful with them. A part of me wanted to tell her the truth. I wanted to yell, "I am losing this battle!" But I just couldn't tell her. She would have been so disappointed and worried, and I would have to face up to what I was doing. I looked away, but in an upbeat tone, I managed to say, "Fine."

"Look at me, Leigh-Ann," Susie said. "Are you really okay?" I said "yes" in that same upbeat tone. She said, "I am not sure I believe you. I don't think you are okay." I got a huge lump in my throat. I couldn't even look at her. She said, "Tell me

what you are doing, what you are eating. Be honest with me."
Tears welled up in my eyes. I tried so hard to fight them back.
The lump in my throat was so large I could hardly swallow. She
said, "I love you. Please tell me what's going on." It took me a
long time to speak. My heart was pounding. I was terrified to
be honest and terrified to lie. Then it all came out.

Susie took my hand and said, "I know you are scared. You
fought me before when I wanted to take you to the hospital.
You aren't going to fight me today. Today is the day, Leigh-Ann.
You must go." I did fight her, giving her every excuse in the
book. "This would hurt Todd terribly," "I have a mother and
daughter shopping day planned with Emily on the weekend,"
"Her birthday is coming up and I am not going to do that to
her. I am not going to miss out and neglect her to go to the
hospital."

She just looked at me and said, "If you don't go today, you
may not be there for her birthday, anyway." I knew what she
meant. I had actually thought about that, too. In my journal a
few days before, I had written:

January 24, 2005
I love seeing the numbers on the scale go down.
What victory I feel. Today I am scared though. I weigh
less than I did when I was going through this twelve
years ago. My reflection scares me. I look like those
pictures of girls with anorexia, but I am not ready to
stop. I know how it affected my body years ago and
I am much older now. I am not sure how much more
my body can take. Physical things are happening. My
period has stopped and I am feeling a pain in my chest.
The vision in my right eye is still blurred. Five or ten
more pounds may be about it. I do sometimes fear that
I won't know I have gotten in so deep that I am losing
my life. I wonder how my electrolytes are. Last night
while vomiting, my chest was hurting so much. I kept

thinking, I don't want to die of a heart attack and do that to Todd and the kids. What if Emily found me in the morning before Todd got home? I can't do that to her, but I can't stop throwing up. I need to get more out of me. I know that thinking is completely selfish and so irrational, but I just can't stop. I feel desperate to get the food out, terrified to keep it in. I slept on the bathroom floor last night. I felt too dizzy and in too much pain to get to bed. Every time I felt better enough to get up, I vomited instead. I feel so scared and afraid. I am paralyzed with fear. I am scared about what may happen if I don't stop, but I am even more terrified to give it up. I had a fleeting thought to call Susie or Todd, but I just couldn't. Then, I would really have to stop. I woke up this morning before Emily and crawled into bed before she came in. Thank goodness she has no idea. What am I doing?

Susie firmly stated, "We are going back to your house to get Todd and then we are going to the hospital." I was mad at her, angry that she was asking me to do this. I was angrier than I think I had ever been at anyone before. She was taking away my security and my control. The drive home was tense. I was upset with her and she knew it. I was afraid to hurt Todd yet again. As I told him my heart broke in two. His eyes were full of fear for the love of his life. I agreed to go to the hospital, but only because I could not look in Todd's eyes and refuse. What was I doing to our marriage, to my husband, and to my children? I had to go. He packed a bag for me and we left for the hospital.

When we arrived at the hospital and told the medical staff all the things I had been doing, they did a chest x-ray and came in to take my blood to check my electrolytes. During the x-ray, I felt dizzy and weak. I knew the feeling. I felt that way many times immediately before I would faint. I asked them if

I could sit down for a minute. When I got back into the room they had me in, they took my blood and gave me an IV. I didn't want the IV. After the nurse left the room, I looked at Todd, began to cry, and pleaded with him to let me go home. He said, "No." I asked again. He said an emphatic, "*No!*" I begged, and he looked at me and said, "I can't lose you. There is no way we are going home until you are better." In between the staff coming and going from the room, Todd, Susie, and I talked. Their unconditional love for me was overwhelming. It was a pure example of God's love for me.

When the resident came in with the test results, he said, "Your labs came back okay, so we can't keep you here. You can go home, but I suggest you go to an in-house treatment center or check into our partial hospitalization program." The program he was referring to was where I would come to the hospital for eight hours a day for group therapy sessions and then go home to be with my family in the evenings.

Todd and I began discussing my options. I didn't want to go to an in-house treatment center out of state, away from my family and support system, and I wasn't sure about this partial hospitalization program. A wave of fear ran through my body. I knew that I would not do well at the partial hospitalization program. I hated group therapy and I knew once I returned home I would freak out from the structure of the day and continue my vomiting. I wanted to vomit just thinking about it.

I am sure Susie read some of what I was thinking. She asked me what my thoughts were. I began to cry and said, "I feel like this was a colossal waste of time. They won't help me, won't admit me because, "good news," there is nothing wrong with me; my labs were fine, but there *is* something wrong with me and I am afraid to go home, afraid of where to go, and don't know if I am ever going to get better."

Looking back now, I have no idea why my labs were okay. That was not a clear indicator of the abuse I had been putting my body through, nor was it permission for me to continue with my addiction. I can only say it was God's protective hand on me, and it instilled enough fear in me to know that I wasn't going to get any help there.

All of this just added to the frustration I was already feeling. But, at some point I had stopped being angry at Todd and Susie for taking me to the hospital, and I knew I needed help. I was scared to leave, but I couldn't stay. So, after eight long hours in the emergency room, we went home. Todd wrote:

> *January 28, 2005*
> *I feel so stupid and naïve that I didn't know how severe this had become. I am frustrated and embarrassed that Susie had to tell me that something was severely wrong with my wife. I trusted Leigh-Ann. I believed her when she said she was doing okay. Maybe that is because I wanted to believe her. I have never experienced her lying to me like this before all this began. God, I know You love Leigh-Ann more than I do. I trust that, but I need her here. I read on the Internet today that 10 percent of all people who have anorexia die from it. I can't lose her. I love her with everything in me, with my whole heart. The kids need her, too. They need their mom to love them and be healthy for them. I need her to help me raise them to know You. She is a great mom. I just can't lose her.*

The next morning I arrived at the partial hospitalization program. *What am I doing here?* I wondered. These people are not like me. They are depressed or suicidal. No one is here for an eating disorder. Just then, a man I recognized came in. He was a group therapist that I had on the floor in the hospital twelve years before. I didn't like him. He was always putting people on the spot and making accusations that were wrong. He said hello to me, told me how the day was run, and then showed me around. He said, "This is all group therapy. You move from group to group and session to session. You are pretty much on your own as long as you follow the schedule. You are on your own for lunch." *Yes!* I thought. The opposite of what I thought it would be. There was actually very little structure to this partial hospitalization program.

I went into the first group. As soon as I walked in, I was confronted by the therapist. I no sooner sat down and she asked, "So why are you here?" Nothing like letting me get comfortable with the people and listen to them talk before I have to spill it all. That just made me mad. I am usually so private about my life and I didn't want to talk. I said what I had to and then it was time to move to the next group. It was the same group of people, same stories, just a different room with a different counselor.

I listened in this group. I heard people who were talking about depression, suicide, medications, self-pity, and even more reasons to feel sorry for themselves. Time was up and we headed to the next room with a different counselor. I found it necessary to take a bathroom break in between. No one noticed. I wanted to throw up and knew no one would know. I started to put my finger down my throat, and then I stopped. I thought of Todd and the kids, and realized there was no turning back. I wanted to get better and I recognized that I could choose to walk away from the temptation. So I went on to the next group, which turned out to be identical to the first two. The same people talked about the same things and, as far as I could tell, no one was accomplishing anything. It was a lot of venting, feeling sorry for self, and comparing of medications. I had had it, but I had told Todd I would try.

Now it was lunchtime, and I hadn't even seen a real doctor yet. I went into the community room and sat by myself. People came and went. No one noticed that I was deliberately skipping lunch. I loved that. I took another bathroom break. The urge to vomit was great. I walked into the bathroom, locked the door behind me, and thought, *I have to throw up*. I started to gag and then I stopped, sat down on the floor, and thought, *Lord, help me to stop this*.

There was an element of desperation in my life. I wanted to live. I wanted to stop hurting myself and be close to God again. I got up, unlocked the door, and walked back to the community room. Again, I recognized that I could choose to walk away from the sin and with His help, I had the strength to do just that. Soon, it was time for yet another group. I sat down with the same group of people, talking about the same things, and wondering how this was helping anyone. There was so much focus on problems instead of solutions. I wondered how these people even functioned in life.

Finally, they called my name to see the psychiatrist. I walked in and explained my situation. I was there five minutes, and he prescribed an anti-depressant. I couldn't believe it. I asked him why he thought I needed an anti-depressant since I wasn't depressed. He said, "It will help you with your urge to throw up and your anxiety with food." I told him that I wanted to try to get better without medication, that I had before and I wanted to try again. He still encouraged me to take it, which bothered me. I knew this wasn't going to work.

Everything in this program was group therapy, but I didn't see how anyone made any progress. I had heard nothing productive all day, and no one there was dealing with what I was. I didn't know how they felt and they didn't know how I felt. There was no structure and no accountability. I had been there for five hours, skipped lunch, and had many opportunities to throw up. I thought my session with the psychiatrist would at least be productive, but after five minutes, all he wanted to do was medicate me. I felt he didn't have enough information to make that kind of assessment. I told him I wanted to leave and he said, "I am sorry that's the way you feel, but it's up to you." I called Todd and left without finishing out my day. Todd wrote:

January 28, 2005
Leigh-Ann called me to pick her up from the hospital
program. She was adamant that it wasn't going to
work. She said, "This place isn't helping. Get me out
of here. Pick me up right now." Here we go again; she
doesn't want to do this or that. She doesn't want to
go on medication, doesn't want to go to the hospital,
doesn't want to go to an in-house treatment center,
but she does want to get better. I think, "How are you
going to do that, then?" How do I know it is not just
another excuse to revert back to her old ways? I am so
frustrated with her.

I left the partial hospitalization program not knowing where to go from there. The way I saw it, I had two options. I could go back to my counselor and do some heavy-duty therapy, or I could go away to a treatment center for eating disorders. I did not want to do the latter. I wanted to be with my family. My counselor strongly urged me to go to the in-house treatment center. But if I chose not to, she agreed to see me as long as I also went to see my family doctor and Todd came to sessions with me. She was skeptical because I was already in therapy and still had spiraled downward. She said the severity of the disorder warranted going to an in-house treatment center, but was willing to let me try it with her first. Todd took the next week off work to stay with me around the clock.

I saw my physician to find out about my chest pain and blurred vision. Thankfully, the chest pain was a pulled muscle from vomiting so much, and in time my vision would return to normal. My doctor casually suggested anti-depressant medication and gave me some literature to read before I made up my mind. I came home and read it, then got on the Internet to find out more. I was still so unsure. Something wasn't right. It wasn't that I was opposed to medication for those who needed it. I knew many people who were on this type of medication, for the right reasons, and it had truly helped them. There was just something unsettling about it in my heart and I could not deny that.

At my next counseling session, my counselor told me that she felt it was necessary for me to be on anti-depressant medication to continue to receive therapy with her. The unsettling feeling in my heart was even stronger. I just couldn't do it. I knew I had anxiety about food, but I was not depressed. I felt that medication, for me in my particular situation, would only be a bandage for the real problem, not the solution. I begged her not to give up on me because I didn't want to take it, but she was firm with her decision. I did not agree. I understand now that she was extremely concerned that I needed more than just outpatient counseling. My Body Mass Index was so low, she was concerned for my life.

Again, she urged me to seek in-house treatment somewhere, which I knew might have to be a possibility at this point, but I wanted another chance to try with family support around me. The thought of leaving my kids was awful. My counselor was firm that if I did not go in-house, and I wanted to continue with her, I had to agree to her terms. I could not, so I left her office that day for the last time.

The moment I left her office, I knew in my heart that medication would be a crutch for me, just as counseling had become. I am certainly not saying that is so for everyone. I know that counseling, particularly Christian counseling, in-house treatment programs, and medication, at the appropriate times, are necessary support tools for the recovery of an eating disorder. Counseling is particularly important to get to the root of the hurt that has caused this underlying pain and to learn how to move past it. Understanding the *why* we choose to control food, use it as a coping mechanism in our lives, getting to the root of our fear and pain is the beginning to finding true freedom. But far too often we are so wrapped up in our own victim mentality, that even well-intended treatment becomes a ploy from the enemy to take our eyes off Christ and focus on the problem. Too many books, counselors, and treatment centers say, "We can help you; we have the key to recovery," but, in reality, God is the only true key to recovery and everything else is just support. It had to be my choice to use the strength He offered. I am not advocating self-therapy or saying that counseling is not necessary, but true healing only comes when "we fix our eyes not on what is seen, but what is unseen. For what is seen is temporary, but what is unseen is eternal" (2 Corinthians 4:18).

Fixing our eyes on Christ, along with counseling, is the best course of action. I had been in and out of counseling for several years and with two different Christian counselors. It was helpful in several ways to identify and work through the pain in my life, but the Lord had shown me that I was leaving Him out of the process. I was failing to realize that He needed to be the foundation of my recovery and He needed to be the priority in my life. God had brought me to a place of surrender and I knew I could not go back. No counselor could give me a better solution to my problem than the one God was offering. First, I needed Him.

Todd was terrified. Now, what were my options? He thought that was my last opportunity for health, unless he could convince me to go away somewhere. The car ride home was silent. I prayed, *Lord, now what? Where do I go from here? How do I get out of this pit?*

My counselor had said once that she saw a pattern in my life. When something goes wrong, I get angry and scared. Being angry with God, trying to be in control of my life, and running from Him, drives me to the edge of the cliff. When I see where I have come, I get scared and run back into the arms of the Father. However, the next time something difficult happens in my life, I get angry and frightened, and I run from Him again, only to get closer to the edge of the cliff each time I visit there.

She said, "Leigh-Ann you are not on the edge of the cliff anymore. You are over the cliff with one hand, hanging on." I knew that was true. I had to make a choice. I was either going to continue to rely on my own strength, which I knew was already failing me, or I had to reach up into the loving arms of my heavenly Father and let Him pull me to safety, never to return to the cliff again.

I prayed silently, *Lord, I want to choose You. I do, but I don't know how to let go of all this anger and fear. Show me how to let You pull me to safety.* He was so faithful to say all the things He had said to me before, that I could not hear then, but could hear so clearly now. Certainly, it was not in an audible voice, but words that filled my spirit and answered all my questions.

He said, "Leigh-Ann, you can be angry with Me, but I will always love you. My love for you is unconditional, unwavering, and all the love you will ever need. That will never change no matter how angry you are with Me. You can be scared, but know that My perfect love casts out all fear. You can run from Me, but I will never leave you nor forsake you. You cannot understand My plan for you. It is not to harm you, but to bring you nearer to Me. I am all the comfort you need in your pain, whether it is physical or emotional. I am all the strength that you need in your weakness against this food addiction and all the peace that you need as you battle what is going on inside of you. I am sufficient for you. Do you *trust* Me? Do you *really trust* Me?"

I thought of a quote that I had read in the book *Every Young Woman's Battle* by Shannon Ethridge and Stephen Arterburn. We happened to be using that book with our youth girls for a sexual purity unit. A sentence remained with me. It said, "When your flesh wrestles with your spirit, do you know who eventually wins? The one you feed the most."[1] I thought, *That's it!* I knew then that my recovery from this food addiction and my acceptance of these health issues, were completely dependent upon my walk with Christ and my ability to trust in His faithfulness to be sufficient for whatever I faced.

I needed to flood my spirit with His Word and to arm myself against the temptations of the enemy. I needed to be at His feet continually and be consumed with the Lord for comfort and strength. I needed to trust in His plan for me and let Him be in control even when life is difficult and I don't understand. I needed to walk closely with Him, so that my will aligned with His and so that I could become an effective tool to be used to glorify Him.

No Longer Afraid

With a new plan in mind, I had lots of work to do, but I felt empowered and I was not afraid anymore. We pulled into the driveway to our home after the long and quiet forty-minute drive and I looked over at Todd. A tear was rolling down the side of his face. He said, "Now what? Where do we go from here?" I said, "It will be okay." He wasn't convinced, and he questioned why I said that when it had not been okay before. I told him I could say that with the same devotion I had when I said our vows on our wedding day; I knew it was going to be okay. Now I knew how to find victory over sin and I was sure that God would give me all that I needed to succeed. I told him what had transpired in my heart with God on the car ride home.

Todd told me he loved me and would help me do this with God's strength. But if I skipped even one meal, or my weight started to drop, then he would insist that I go back for professional help. I agreed and thanked him for giving me a chance to try by using God's strength. My husband was my support and my accountability. He took off work, made my meals, sat with me while I ate them, and after I ate them. He helped me keep a food journal, weighed me without me knowing what the number was, controlled when and how long I could be on the treadmill, talked to me about my feelings, and prayed with me. It seemed much like a parent-child relationship. I knew it was unfair for me to ask this of him. I told him how he was truly living out our vows, "in sickness and in health."

I asked him how he was feeling with it all. He said, "Leigh-Ann, I am not doing this only out of commitment. I am doing this because I love you and can't watch you slip away from me. I need you in my life, so to take off work, make a few meals, and enjoy your company is not too much to ask." I cherished what the Lord had given me in my husband and felt like I was the luckiest woman alive. His love was completely unconditional and forgiving, such a pure example of God. He wrote:

> *February 1, 2005*
> *I feel like I am in this nightmare that is never going to be over, never going to end. Nothing is helping. I can't lose her. Again she says, "Trust me." She says she knows how to fight this. I am not convinced, but nothing else is working. I hope she does rely on God and somehow she gets better. I have to give her the chance. At the hospital, they said her labs were currently okay, so I have a little time to let her try, but I know that doesn't mean she is fine. She's not. I am going to take off two weeks and spend every moment with her, make her meals, encourage her to eat, and then sit with her afterward to make sure she isn't throwing it up. I know I am not a counselor, but she seems motivated to try this with God's help so I need to support her in that and encourage her as much as I can. I love her. I know her better than anyone else and have more invested in her life than someone who doesn't know her, doesn't love her, and doesn't really care. I have to try to help her and be there for her. She needs me. This is something I have to do. The only way for her to get better is if the food goes in and stays in. Her physical body needs to be nourished first. Her health has to be stabilized, and then we can worry*

about doing it on her own. I want to help her as much as I can, but I can only do so much. I can't make her eat. She has to want to try and want to completely fight this. I wonder if she is ready to give it over to God. If she is, I know God will help her through this. I know He is the answer. She seems different this time. When I talk to her about how she is feeling, she is honest with me for the first time and doesn't have that nervous laugh. Being home with her and talking her through it will hopefully break this cycle of secrecy and deceit she has fallen into. If she knows how much I love her, and knows that she is not disappointing me, then maybe she can begin to be really honest with me about all of this and work through what is at the source of her pain.

At first, almost every moment was a struggle. I had to keep reminding myself that the Lord is the most wonderful counselor of all, and to just rely on His Spirit, rest in His comfort, and trust in His faithfulness. There were some days that were ugly. One of the first days after the trip to the ER and walking out of counseling, Todd made me breakfast. I didn't want to eat it. I already had enough of "eating right," which was really so minimal. On this day, he made me two eggs and a piece of toast. I told him I didn't want it. He encouraged me to eat. I said, "No." He asked me to eat just a little. I said, "No!" He pleaded with me to eat, just one bite. I said, *"No!"* I started to cry and said, "I can't do it.

I picked up the dishtowel that was lying on the table next to me and threw it across the room. He came over to comfort me and I pushed him away. I told him I couldn't do it, and he reminded me that I could do it with God's strength. Tears streamed down my face. He took my hand and we began to pray. He asked for the Lord's strength to be upon me. We talked about the Scripture from Matthew 6:25: "Therefore, I tell you, do not worry about what you will eat or drink; or about your body, what you will wear. Is not life more important than food, and the body more important than clothes?"

Then Todd said, "Leigh-Ann, rely on that. Go on autopilot. Just eat, don't think, don't worry, just give it to God. Trust in Him and take baby steps." We started talking about other things, so my mind would be distracted, and soon I had finished several bites and half of the piece of toast. And I kept it down. Todd continued to journal:

> *February 5, 2005*
> *I am frustrated and angry. Why is she fighting me to eat? She got so upset she threw a towel at me just because I was encouraging her to take a bite. I know this is hard for her. I just put my arms around her and reminded her of how much I loved her. I knew I had to encourage her. I knew we had to pray and then I reminded her of what Matthew 6:25 says about not worrying. We are just going to have to take very small baby steps.*

I knew this battle was going to be tough. I knew Satan wasn't going to give up just because I acknowledged that the Lord was with me. In fact, I thought Satan might try even harder to get me to fall. And that's just what he did.

Journal Questions

1. How do you believe you are being sifted?

2. Read 1 Corinthians 10:13. Do you believe the promise that God never gives someone more than they can handle? What does that mean to you?

3. Do you find yourself feeling comfort and fear at the same time? How is that possible? What is the source of your comfort? If your comfort is not from God, will it last? If your comfort is from God, how then can you be feeling fear?

4. Have you made attempts at recovery and failed? What did that look like and why did you fail?

5. Read Matthew 6:25. What is this verse saying to you? In what areas do you need to apply it to your life?

Prayer

Dear Heavenly Father,

Help me to see that the comfort I get from food is not lasting, that it's a false comfort, and that true comfort only comes from You. Help me to trust in Your comfort and not be afraid. Lord, as You allow Satan to sift me, as You refine my heart, I pray that I will seek You more. I know that true freedom only comes through You. Amen.

CHAPTER 11

The Battle Between Flesh and Spirit

When your flesh wrestles with your spirit, do you know who will eventually win? Whichever one you feed the most.[1]

Finally, be strong in the Lord and in his mighty power. Put on the full armor of God so that you can take your stand against the devil's schemes. For our struggle is not against flesh and blood, but against the rulers, against the authorities, against the powers of this dark world and against the spiritual forces of evil in the heavenly realms. (See Ephesians 6:10-12).

As I began recovery in early February 2005, it was apparent that this truly was a battle. It was a war within me and against the enemy who tried desperately to fulfill his purpose to destroy me, to pull me away from Christ, and to make me completely ineffective for God. Satan began his manipulation, yet again. He was, and is, sly and cunning. He tried whatever it would take to keep my focus off Christ and on the weakest areas of my life: anger, fear, being in control, and food.

In the past, I had spent countless hours reading books on eating disorders and eating healthy. The more attention and focus I placed on food, the more it remained an issue. That is exactly where Satan wanted to keep me. My focus was on food or the way I looked every second of every day, which left no time to focus on Christ. What I read simply talked about getting a better body image and eating healthy, or it came from a psychological standpoint of what needed to change in my personality to get better. None of this was helpful to me. I had been there, done that, and was still struggling. None of these books dealt with issues of the heart that were at the root of my problem, like anger and fear. Some mentioned a desire to control or a need for love and acceptance, but none of them led me back to Christ for all the answers I needed.

At some point, I realized that I had to pick up the Bible and the kind of books that revealed more of who Christ is—those that would promote my spiritual growth. That became my best defense. I dove in without looking back and began to feed my spirit. One thing for sure, the truth about my disorder was starting to come to light. The truth is that there is a direct correlation between my walk with God, my knowledge of who He is, and my freedom from this addiction. I had to examine my heart, recognize my sin, and focus on the power found in Christ. Practically, what did that look like?

The Truth About My Disorder

I think when someone is in the midst of this type of addiction, or any addiction for that matter, they can't see clearly how this truly affects them. When I took a good, honest look at my life as I began my recovery, I was horrified, shocked at the place to which I had come. I used the eating disorder as a coping mechanism for anytime my life got tough, out of my control, or when I felt like a failure. It was something I knew I was good at controlling and would support my desire for perfection. Getting an internal rush when someone would say, "You're losing weight" or needing a smaller size of clothing or watching the numbers on the scale decrease made me feel in complete control. That is what initially gave me comfort, but it was a false comfort. At some point, and, again, I was unaware of when it really happened, the control I thought I had gave way to sacrificing everything to submit to the temptation. I truly felt powerless against it. The eating disorder had kept me enslaved to my anger and fear, and it kept me from finding my true value and worth in Christ. At one point I specifically remember recognizing that I was not in control; that this really was a battle. If I was enslaved to this sin, then Satan was in control and if I was submissive to God, then He was. I was either motivated by the Spirit or motivated by temptation, but I still had the power to choose which voice I was going to listen to. I became exhausted with fighting this internal battle over and over again.

Looking into the mirror honestly showed a reflection of this monster in my life that just kept taking from me, stripping me of righteousness, and filling me with sin. To maintain this addiction, I had to lie, deceive, hide, and be completely selfish. I was no longer a woman of integrity, but a master at manipulation and selfishness. This sin was directly affecting the relationships all around me, including my relationship with my Father in Heaven.

I had compromised so much to remain in sin. I had hurt, lied to, and deceived my husband and friends. It had become natural for me to want to cover up, deceive, and manipulate so that I could starve myself and vomit. That manipulation only put me further from recovery and further from my husband, my children, my friends, and my relationship with God. It drove a wedge between me and anyone who cared about me.

I became great at lying and manipulating. Hiding was what I naturally wanted to do, but I also knew that there would come a time when everyone would find out the truth, anyway. Matthew 10:26 tells us, "There is nothing concealed that will not be disclosed, or hidden that will not be made known."

I knew it would only be a matter of time before my thinning body became evident to all.

My marriage was no longer based on trust, but a fear of becoming known for what I had become. I had pulled away from all my friends, closed into myself, and become a poor example of Christ to my children, youth girls, and anyone else Christ brought into my life. I knew the enemy could not have my soul. I already belonged to Christ, but Satan sure kept me focused on self, oblivious to serving others' needs, and ineffective in furthering God's kingdom.

Sometimes I think the enemy works harder at keeping Christians in sin than he does non-Christians. When he can immobilize God's hands and feet, then he has accomplished his task by preventing growth in Christians and keeping the souls of non-believers that much longer.

I knew that my well-being and what I was doing wasn't just about me. No one sins in a vacuum. Deep in my heart I wanted this all to be over. I wanted to be close to God and my husband again, and I wanted more than anything to be a good example for my children and to be used by God. Since this wasn't just about me, I had to stop thinking that way. I had to ask myself if it was really that important to *feel* like I was in control and jeopardize every important relationship in my life. This addiction was robbing me of everything I really wanted—health, joy, closeness with my family, a strong relationship with God, and being an effective tool for Him.

Choices

Every day we make thousands of choices. In fact, we make choices within each moment about what we say, what we do, and how we act and react to others or to the situations we face. Lasting recovery and true freedom are really based on what we choose in these moments and who we choose to listen to. The very first and most important choice I had to make in my recovery was to admit there was a problem, and ask myself if I really wanted to be healthy, even if that meant doing what was contrary to what I naturally wanted to do. Could I deny self and give everything over to God? Did I want to follow Him no matter what that looked like? Did I trust Him enough to let go of my control? The real question at hand was, "Am I willing to do what it takes, to sit at God's feet, to learn more about Him and to ultimately deny self?" not "Will God supply what I need?" His Word is clear about His provision of strength and comfort in our time of need (see Scripture verses at the end of the chapter). It is ironic that God promises to provide for our every need if we trust Him, and yet we hold on to what is hurting us and continue to choose our own way even when it robs us of what we really want. So few of us are willing to do what it really takes to let go. I was at a crossroad in my recovery where what I was learning about God had to transfer from knowledge in my head to belief in my heart, and finally to action in my life. I knew that I only had two choices. It was that point on the edge of the cliff. I was either going to follow God, which meant giving over everything, trusting enough to let go, and reach up for Him to take my hand; or I could continue to go my own way, which would only lead me down a path of more destruction and a fall to my doom. This choice would be the most difficult choice I had ever made, but I knew it was a choice that meant getting better. A life of walking with God, a healthy life, and a life of trusting in Him would be the reward. Looking at my life I realized that in the past I had royally messed up by doing it my own way. Doing what I wanted to do, what seemed natural, and being in control led to complete disaster. This, I knew, would please the enemy. I had to choose. I had to search my heart to see if I was truly at the point of surrender, letting God have it all, and trusting Him. Finally I was at that point, so I had to make another choice … the choice to face my sins and ask for help.

The deception had to stop. It was only hurting my marriage, especially now when my husband was trying to help me. I desperately wanted to be a woman of integrity again. The change had to begin in my heart. I knew the enemy wanted me to feel like I had no other options but to lie, so I forced myself to be completely honest from that point on, even if it meant upsetting those who loved me, or my sin being discovered. I had to do what I was most afraid of. I had to tell my husband *everything*. I had to choose to be honest at every crossroad, at every fear, at every desire to control.

Part of that honesty was telling him exactly how I was feeling and that I was afraid. Todd was trying to help me; to continue to lie to him would get me nowhere in my recovery. He was watching me waste away and he was scared, too. We were now in this fight together. Being completely honest with him was the first step, and the beginning to rebuilding the trust in our marriage. I had to begin that process with my friends to restore those relationships, as well. Todd journaled.

> *February 16, 2005*
> *I feel a lot better now then when Leigh-Ann was lying to me. I am scared when she tells me she is struggling, but at least now we can deal with it and it is not like the elephant in the room that no one can talk about. At least I know now she is serious about it. She is upset when she fails, messes up, or has irrational thoughts. She just needs help and support through it. I still want to believe her, but my judgment was flawed before so I am not sure if I can rely completely on what I think, so I am weighing her with her back turned to the scale. I need to know for sure how she is doing and that is the only concrete evidence I have. I can tell she is really trying. She is much more open and honest with how she feels about things. She never talked to me about it before and now I feel like we are working it out together.*

Beginning to be completely honest was a huge step in the battle against the enemy because it required great accountability. If I had made the commitment to be honest with all those in my life, then the last thing I wanted to do was to have to say that I was submitting to the temptation and hurting myself again. I knew this would only hurt me and those who loved me. That became a huge deterrent from being in sin.

I knew that accountability was a huge factor, so in addition to Todd, I had Susie be my accountability partner. She prayed for and with me, and she checked up on me daily to ensure I was staying on track. This accountability was huge in breaking the pattern of secrecy and lies. I could no longer hide. I want to just say here that accountability is essential. Physically, I had Todd sit with me while I ate and be with me after I ate early on in my recovery, so I had support in following through with what I knew was right. Spiritually, I had Susie and another close friend of mine praying for me daily, checking on my progress, and listening when I needed to talk.

I suggest that you find a few strong believers in your life who can speak truth over you and be an authority in your life to help support you when you need it the most—early in your recovery. If you do not have that, and are still failing at walking away from those temptations, then I suggest you seek full-time professional support such as an in-house treatment center (resources are given at the end of the book). Those centers are great at supporting and assisting you with recovery, but remember the change must first be in you. It must be your choice to follow God and use His strength to fight the enemy, or when you leave you will only revert back to your old ways. That kind of help and support is temporary; you must learn to do this on your own, with God, or it is not true recovery and lasting freedom.

Powerless Against the Enemy Is a Lie—
Finding Strength in Christ

Accountability was a huge factor in my recovery, but there were so many times that I still felt powerless in this battle. I felt like I couldn't be strong and that I couldn't walk away from the temptation when I didn't have support systems around. Satan held me at bay. He wanted me to believe that I was powerless against his strength. That is right where the enemy wanted me. If I stayed there, then everything in my wonderful life, all the blessings that God had given me, would be compromised just so I could have control.

The truth was that it was only an illusion that I had control, when, in fact, Satan did. He had me away from God, hurting myself, hurting my family, and being an ineffective tool. This is not what I wanted, but I truly believed that I had no fight left. Who was I to think that I could fight the enemy alone? Trying to fight him by myself was getting me no-where and I had become completely exhausted with the fight. I wanted to give up. It was easier to just give in. It just seemed too hard.

Somehow, that quote kept ringing in my ear "the one that always wins is the one you feed the most." I thought, okay, my victory over this sin depends on my ability to feed my spirit. One thing to know about me, I am a completely stubborn and strong-willed person. Once I have set my mind to something, then I go after it full force, hence the reason my eating disorder was so serious. I decided to use all that energy that I had once used to destroy myself to be completely submerged in Christ. I had to go into the battle with the full armor that God provided. I wrote in my journal:

> *February 10, 2005*
> *I have decided that hiding and lying are no longer options. I have been completely honest with Todd about everything and will continue to be so. I am glad I have accountability to keep me from hiding. I am so sorry that*

I have hurt him that way. I wish I could take it all back, but I can't. I just have to continue to be honest with him now. Oh, Lord, this battle is so difficult. Sometimes I feel so powerless against these temptations to not eat, but why give up now? I am upset that I have spent so much time and energy wasted on hurting myself and that Satan has had a foothold in my life for so long. I have been allowing him to win. Why? I'm gonna fight him. I'm gonna fight him with all I've got. I am going to use that time and energy to feed my spirit and sit at your feet. I know I am strong enough to beat this, but only with You. I need You. I need Your strength in this fight Lord. I can't do it on my own; that is clear. I have been failing at it for twenty years. I want freedom, please, show me how. I remember what You have told me, that You are all my comfort in my pain and all the strength in my weakness and all my peace in this battle.

I knew that no matter how much the enemy tried to keep his hold on me, God was still the authority. Satan's power paled in comparison to that of my Almighty Father. The Lord showed me how to fight with His strength and with the armor He provided (Ephesians 6:14-17), and ultimately find the freedom I so desired. Feeding my spirit meant finding out who God really was in my life and correcting my skewed view of Him. It meant reading His Word to develop a proper perspective of Him and it meant sitting at His feet consistently to hear His voice. Knowing Him better made it easier to trust, make the right choices, relinquish control, believe in His plan, experience His unconditional love, and rely on His strength. This battle was so hard. My own natural desire was to do it my way, but God reminded me of His promise that no matter what He placed in my life, He would give me His strength to endure. 1 Corinthians 10:13 says, "No temptation has seized you except what is common to man. And God is faithful; he will not let you be tempted beyond what you can bear. But when you are tempted, he will also provide a way out so that you can stand up under it." God is faithful. I had to believe that. He wanted me to overcome this, but I had to recognize how much I needed Him to do that. Ephesians 6:16 says, "Taking up the shield of faith with which you will be able to extinguish all the flaming missiles of the evil one." God was showing me clearly that just my faith could defeat the enemy, and yet He provided more.

Power in God's Word

I began to arm myself against the enemy with God's Word—the sword of the Spirit. At this point, I recognized that my irrational thoughts were, in fact, lies from Satan. That was his ploy to take me out. Each lie he told was like artillery shot directly at me. I began to journal all my thoughts about eating. In so doing, I could go back and read what I had written and separate rational feelings from irrational thoughts. As I did, I saw that there was a pattern in my thinking, issues with anger, fear, trusting God, control, and self-worth. They had been constant my entire life.

When life became difficult, Satan would use those difficulties to bring me down. I remembered that when the Lord was tempted in the desert, He used Scripture to fight the enemy (see Luke 4:1-13). So, now, whatever lies Satan was telling me, I found Scripture to directly combat those lies. It became my armor. I wrote them down in my journal right next to my irrational thoughts. I began to hide God's Word in my heart so that as soon as I started to hear those lies in my head, I could draw from God's Word, which would tell me the truth.

Psalm 119:9-16 says:

How can a young man keep his way pure? By living according to your word. I seek you with all my heart; do not let me stray from your commands. I have hidden your word in my heart that I may not sin against you. Praise be to you, O Lord; teach me your decrees. With my lips I recount all the laws that come from your mouth. I rejoice in following your statutes as one rejoices in great riches. I meditate on your precepts and consider your ways. I delight in your decrees; I will not neglect your word.

I no longer neglected God's Word, but realized how much power it had to speak truth in my life and over the lies the enemy was feeding me.

Power in Prayer

Arming myself with God's Word was huge. It was a great defense against the enemy each time he tried to bring me down. I knew that he was powerful and I needed more strength in my fight against him. Unlike other addictions, I couldn't just walk away from food or eating and eliminate it from my life. I had to face it at least three times each day, and I was having huge problems with that. I had starved my body for so long that I really no longer felt hunger. I couldn't decipher natural cues that the Lord had given me to tell me that I was hungry and when I was satisfied. I also couldn't differentiate when my body really did need food or if I just wanted food. I couldn't make good choices about when, what, and how much to consume. I know that sounds strange, but if you are there, in the midst of it, you know what I mean. I truly had no idea how to eat. Food had become an anesthetic, a coping mechanism, an area to control, and I didn't know how to see it merely as nourishment for my body. I desperately needed wisdom from the Lord.

Praying for Strength

Jesus had told His disciples in the Garden of Gethsemane to "'Watch and pray so that you will not fall into temptation. The spirit is willing, but the body is weak'" (Matthew 26:41). I decided to pray for strength. I had to choose to become consistent in my prayer life and sitting at God's feet, not just randomly throw my requests to Him. My prayerful heart was continual, almost a true *praying without ceasing*. I needed His comfort in my pain and His strength in my weakness against this food addiction. When I woke up in the morning, my first feeling and thought was of pain from my Interstitial Cystitis. Since I faced my pain all day long, that became my cue. When I felt pain, I would pray for strength for that and wisdom in my eating. I began my day by praying for my pain to be minimal or bearable, and if it wasn't, to remember to rest in the comfort of Him. Then I prayed that my eating would be nourishing to my body and glorifying to the Lord. I prayed continually throughout the day when I felt pain and then again at each time I should eat.

I prayed each time I was faced with food. I prayed for peace to begin eating. I prayed for wisdom in what to eat, a clear indication that I had had enough, but not too much, and strength to stop when I was satisfied. Understanding my body's cues took a long time, but I wasn't going to be able to recognize them if I wasn't praying first. It seemed like it had been forever since I had eaten normally. Knowing when and how much to eat wasn't going to happen for me overnight, especially since it had been a long time since I had even felt hunger. Jumping into eating without arming myself with God's strength through prayer was like a runner beginning a marathon without stretching or a student taking a test without studying or a soldier entering battle without his weapons. I knew that would set me up for failure. I also realized that when I prayed, it had to be with everything I had in me. I couldn't pray half-heartedly or pray and then not listen to His voice and to what He was telling me. I needed God. I needed to depend on Him, to remain on my knees to feel at peace as I began to gain weight, and to remain stable with my eating. I had to pray; then act.

More Choices

I knew that the Holy Spirit would guide me, but I also knew that it was up to me to choose to follow Him and use His strength or be led astray by the enemy's voice. I prayed for the Lord's voice to be strong, so strong it would drown out the enemy's and that I would ultimately eat within God's will. I learned to be still, to stop talking, and begin listening. Then, I was obedient to what He was telling me.

> *Do not merely listen to the word, and so deceive yourselves. Do what it says. Anyone who listens to the word but does not do what it says is like a man who looks at his face in the mirror and, after looking at himself, goes away and immediately forgets what he looks like. But the man who looks intently into the perfect law that gives freedom, and continues to do this, not forgetting what he has heard, but doing it—he will be blessed in what he does. (James 1:22-25)*

For many, this is where the disconnect comes. Do they want health? Yes. Do they say with their lips, "I want to give this over to God?" Yes. But are they willing to do what is necessary for true health? Are they willing to do the work to be at God's feet and to find strength in Him? Some girls I have worked with have said, "Yes, I know I need to do that, but how can I?" "How can God really make me better?" "How is this really practical and helpful advice?" "God doesn't verbally speak back and He doesn't make me eat or make me walk away from the toilet." "This is just too hard." "This fight seems impossible." "I just want to give up." Here is the reality: God works in the impossible. He makes the impossible, possible. It seemed impossible for David to fight Goliath, but in the end who reigned in victory? You can find strength in Him by trusting Him and by choosing to be with Him. You hear His voice more clearly when you are with Him consistently and you are better equipped to walk away from temptation when you desire to do His will more than you desire your own. Try spending time with Him, at His feet, and see what a difference it begins to make in your life.

Power in Praise

I had spent so much time wallowing in my own self-pity, focused on what I couldn't do, and in fear of trying, that I really was preventing God from helping me. One day as I was sitting at God's feet, I began to sing praise and worship songs. The tune in my heart that was radiating from my lips was so beautiful—thankfulness for a God who loves me, joy to serve a God who is my strength and refuge, and a desire to know Him more. I looked at the blessings in my life, the gifts He has given me, and found the comfort and strength I had been longing for. The blessings that I focused on were not the material things in my life, but the gifts He has given me: forgiveness and grace, a relationship with Him, a promise of unconditional love, and life everlasting. I sang out loud in praise and adoration. I sang out strong in faith and trust. I sang out confident in His love. I sang out and found power to overcome. I found that thankfulness and praise were a mighty sword against temptation and a tool to change the momentum of a fearful, angry, and pity-full heart.

As I began to give everything over to God and sit at His feet in prayer and praise, moment by moment, it became easier to follow Him and hear His voice. I was able to feel and recognize hunger. I could decipher the cues He was giving me and recognize when I needed to eat. I began to make wise food choices and feel good about nourishing my body. Being with God, in His presence, was a great defense against the enemy.

To this day, I still need to be on my knees. Now, it is just an overall awareness of wanting to walk with Christ. If I am not praying or walking with Him consistently, then I am struggling with my eating and giving Satan a foothold. This is something that I will always deal with. Eating, along with my physical pain, are truly, the thorns in my flesh. Unlike my pain, though, the eating disorder was something I initially chose, but God was using it to show me that I must remain in Him. Now I was making conscious choices to follow Him, use His strength, and praise Him for His work in my life. Of course, it isn't such a painful struggle now. It is more like an awareness of dependency, something I know I can't do on my own. I am still on my knees about what I eat, and if I start to overeat, or overeat junk food, then I stop to pray for wisdom and strength.

Some might say that it sounds like I am still locked within my food prison. On the contrary, this is something that arms me against the enemy and keeps me walking closely with God and continually at His feet. I recognize my need for a prayerful heart to stay in God's will about my eating. There is so much freedom in trusting in Him and using His strength to fight my battles. The roller coaster I was on could only stop on its tracks when I became consistent with my walk, and going to Him regularly for strength. My ride soon began to look like a slow and steady incline, instead of a rapid rise and fall.

Power in Obedience to Christ and Trusting Him

I started to realize that the things I had held onto—to feel in control or give me comfort—were also footholds for the enemy. They aided him in this battle and were things that I desperately had to rid myself of and give over to God. As long as I held onto my control factors, those things that gave me comfort, my crutches, I would continue to yo-yo in my recovery. It was as if I was saying, "Here, God, you can be in control except for these things—checking my weight, examining my body, exercising, and eating only safe foods."

I knew God was asking me to lay everything at His feet and trust Him. It was like I could almost verbally hear Him say, "Leigh-Ann, do you *trust* Me? Do you *really trust* Me?" Until I could do that, Satan would always have the reins. Giving up these things was terrifying to me. How would I be okay with eating if I had to eat things I wasn't comfortable with? How would I be okay with not knowing how much I weighed? How would I be okay with not over-exercising? These things, in my mind, made it okay to eat and still kept me in control. I knew God loved me and didn't want me unhealthy, but I had to trust Him and allow Him to work.

And Yet More Choices

There was a point when I had to make the decision to let go of what was hurting me and make wise choices continually through my day. There was not room enough in my life for both myself and God to be on the throne. Remaining in control and holding onto these comfort factors, kept Christ from being the center of my life. I could no longer live with one foot in each world. Daily choices to relinquish control and walk away from temptation were clear indicators of growth and progress in my recovery.

I knew I had to get rid of my scale. It was a stumbling block for me. There was so much power in the number. It had become the gauge in my life of success or failure. Todd hid it. I must admit that at first I searched for it, feeling like my security blanket had just been taken away. I weighed in on a weekly basis with both Todd and my doctor, but I turned my back, never looked, and never knew the number that was registering my success or failure. At first, it was so hard not to know, but as I continued in my recovery and in trusting God, I didn't need to ask if it had been a good week. I already knew that if I had been praying and trusting, then no matter what the number was, I had been successful. I had to choose to walk away from, or not look at the scale when it was available, or remove it from my home.

For awhile, I had to stop exercising. As healthy as exercising is, it was still something that kept me in control and set me up for failure. It had become another crutch. I knew I couldn't just cut back to a reasonable amount. I had to give it over to

Him completely. It was as if I needed to over-exercise. It gave me permission to eat. If I prayed to trust Him with what I was eating and then went ahead and exercised after I ate, there was no trust involved. I still controlled what I was doing and I wasn't depending on Him.

For a time, I had to choose not to exercise at all. Then I slowly reintroduced it back into my life because I knew that exercise, done in the right way, with the right mindset, was taking care of the body that God had created. Slowly, I began a few times a week and only with the mindset of wanting to, not having to. I also had to make wise decisions about what kind of exercise to do because of my health problems. In the past, the amount and type of exercise I was engaged in made my pain excruciating. I had to make good decisions about taking care of my whole body, exercising to strengthen my muscles, and not increasing my daily pain. Now, I know that if my exercise becomes ritualistic, harmful, or ceases to be fun, then I am doing it for the wrong reasons. I have to stop until my focus is right again.

I also had in my mind a list of foods that were okay, safe foods to eat. These foods included no fat, no sugar, high-protein types of foods and fresh vegetables. I knew if I ate these foods, I would remain in control of my weight. I didn't have a problem with them and it gave me comfort to know how many calories I was consuming. I also knew what foods to avoid so I wouldn't binge. Again, being in control like this made it okay to eat. There was no trusting in God involved. I knew that this method also had to go. I had to stop counting calories, stop yo-yo-ing between restriction and binge eating, and begin to reintroduce foods that I was afraid of. I had to focus on the nourishment they were giving my body, instead of how many calories I was consuming, and eat foods that I had previously binged on in moderation. Slowly, but surely, at each meal I would eat something I knew I needed, and that would force me to trust Him. I had to choose to trust Him, choose to eat healthy, and keep it down.

Actually, what the enemy wanted me to believe was completely false. I was not powerless. I held the keys to open my prison door. It was up to me to use those keys. My whole heart had to be in it. If I prayed, asking the Lord to give me strength, but then I decided to restrict, or overeat and purge, continue to over-exercise, check my weight, or exert control in some other way to give me comfort, then I had not prayed to defeat the enemy. I had to choose to give it all over and to remain on my knees with my whole heart devoted to Him.

I had to decide whether or not I was going to remain on the throne, letting Satan win, or lay it *all* at God's feet and let Him reign in my life, even if being out of control was the most terrifying thing I had ever faced. I had to fight. I refused to let Satan tell me I was powerless, when in fact, with God I had everything I needed to defeat the enemy and win this struggle. I knew exactly what to do to be victorious in this battle.

Initially, relinquishing my control was one of the hardest things I have ever had to do. It terrified me to not be in control and to have to completely trust God, but in the end I realized just how freeing that was. I had to change my heart before it felt good to let go of that control. I had to trust in what I knew about God. He loves me, He is faithful, and He wants me healthy. Focusing on that made giving over my control and choosing to make the right decision so much easier.

Once I placed everything at God's feet, I found rest and peace in Him. There was tremendous strength in that. What I was most afraid of—relinquishing my control and relying on Him completely—now gave me so much comfort and so much power against the enemy. It diffused Satan's power and gave me strength. I no longer felt powerless and knew that God had supplied me with all that I needed to find victory in this battle between flesh and spirit. Sinclair Ferguson writes in his book *A Heart for God*, "The God who has the power to create the world in which we live has the power to sustain us in our weakness." [12]

My suggestion is to spend a block of time (a day, two days, even a week) just at God's feet. Pray, praise, study His Word, and keep a journal, if you like. Just be with Him and see how peace, comfort, and strength overflow into your life. Discover how His voice can be heard, how His Word can bring truth and how His power can overcome.

When Daniel was faced with being thrown into the lion's den for not praying to King Darius, he retreated to a high room to be alone with God and pray (Daniel 6:6-10). Scripture says he sat in praise and thanksgiving. David, when surrounded by enemies, battles, and opposition, repeatedly went to the Lord for wisdom and discernment, comfort and strength (2 Samuel 5:19,23 and 7:18-29). Jesus regularly spent solitude time with His Father: praying before He chose His twelve apostles (Mark 1:35-39, Luke 6:12); during the Transfiguration (Mark 9:2-12 and Luke 9:28); for comfort and strength in His distress before His death (Mark 14:32-41 and Luke 22:39-45). He warned His disciples to pray so they would not fall into temptation. What great examples of how we should be sitting at God's feet in praise and thanksgiving. Praying in the midst of hardship, for wisdom and discernment when faced with opposition, and in making decisions. Praying to be changed, for comfort and strength in distress and sorrow, and that we won't fall into temptation.

Additional Helpful Scripture

Hiding God's Word in My Heart
Psalm 119:105: "Your word is a lamp to my feet and a light for my path."

Fear

Psalm 46:1-2: "God is our refuge and strength, an ever-present help in trouble. Therefore we will not fear, though the earth give way and the mountains fall into the heart of the sea ..."

Hebrews 13:5-6: "'Never will I leave you; Never will I forsake you.' So we say with confidence, 'The Lord is my helper; I will not be afraid.'"

Trust

Psalm 13:5-6: "But I trust in your unfailing love; my heart rejoices in your salvation. I will sing to the Lord, for He has been good to me."

Psalm 143:8: "Let the morning bring me word of your unfailing love, for I have put my trust in you. Show me the way I should go, for to you I lift up my soul."

Isaiah 12:2: "Surely God is my salvation; I will trust and not be afraid. The Lord, the Lord, is my strength and my song; he has become my salvation."

Luke 8:22-25: "One day Jesus said to his disciples, 'Let's go over to the other side of the lake.' So they got into a boat and set out. As they sailed, he fell asleep. A squall came down on the lake, so that the boat was being swamped, and they were in great danger. The disciples went and woke him saying, 'Master, Master, we're going to drown!' He got up and rebuked the wind and raging waters; the storm subsided and all was calm. 'Where is your faith?' he asked his disciples. In fear and amazement they asked one another, 'Who is this? He commands even the wind and the water, and they obey him.'"

1 Corinthians 10:13: "No temptation has seized you except what is common to man. And God is faithful; he will not let you be tempted beyond what you can bear. But when you are tempted, he will also provide a way out so that you can stand up under it."

Suffering

Exodus 3:7-8: "The Lord said, 'I have indeed seen the misery of my people in Egypt. I have heard them crying out because of their slave drivers, and I am concerned about their suffering. So I have come down to rescue them from the hand of the Egyptians …'"

Exodus 13:20-22: "After leaving Succoth they camped at Etham on the edge of the desert. By day the Lord went ahead of them in a pillar of cloud to guide them on their way and by night in a pillar of fire to give them light, so that they could travel by day or by night. Neither the pillar of cloud by day nor the pillar of fire by night left its place in front of the people."

Job 36:15: "But those who suffer he delivers in their suffering; he speaks to them in their affliction."

Isaiah 49:13: "For the Lord comforts his people and will have compassion on his afflicted ones."

Jeremiah 29:11-14: "'For I know the plans that I have for you,' declares the Lord, 'plans to prosper you and not to harm you, plans to give you hope and a future. Then you will call upon me and come and pray to me, and I will listen to you. You will seek me and find me when you seek me with all your heart. I will be found by you,' declares the Lord, 'and will bring you back from captivity. I will gather you from all the nations and places where I have banished you,' declares the Lord, 'and will bring you back to the place from which I carried you into exile.'"

Romans 5:3: "... we also rejoice in our sufferings, because we know that suffering produces perseverance ..."

Following God

Psalm 37:7: "Be still before the Lord and wait patiently for him."

Romans 8:5: "Those who live according to the sinful nature have their minds set on what that nature desires; but those who live in accordance with the Spirit have their minds set on what the Spirit desires."

Romans 12:1-2: "Therefore I urge you, brothers, in view of God's mercy, to offer your bodies as living sacrifices, holy and pleasing to God—this is your spiritual act of worship. Do not conform any longer to the pattern of this world, but be transformed by the renewing of your mind. Then you will be able to test and approve what God's will is—his good, pleasing and perfect will."

Journal Questions

1. Do you believe there is a battle going on?

2. What does the battle look like in your life?

3. How have you become ineffective for God?

4. Do you need to change your focus?

5. What is the truth about your disorder?

6. When you truly look at your life at present: Where has the false comfort taken you? Have you chosen to lie, deceive, and manipulate to feed your obsession with control? What do the relationships in your life look like? Who have you hurt, pushed away, lied to? Who has your eating disorder driven a wedge between? Who else is affected by your eating disorder? Has the control given way to sacrificing what you truly want in life?

7. Who do you trust that can hold you accountable and speak the truth in love?

8. Do you believe that you are powerless in this battle? Why or why not?

9. What will it take for you to fight this addiction and the enemy?

10. Truthfully answer, "Am I willing to do what it takes to find freedom?"

11. Do you believe that God supplies all that you need? Why or why not?

12. Where is your heart? Who have you chosen to listen to and follow?

13. Read Psalm 119:9-16 and then read the Scripture verses at the end of this chapter. Which verses are speaking to you that you need to hide in your heart?

14. Read Matthew 26:41. How can you strengthen your prayer life, the study of God's Word, and make praise and worship time a consistent part of your day?

15. Do you believe that a huge part of recovery is relinquishing your control factors? How does that make you feel? What do you need to relinquish control of? Make a list. Refer back to Question 3 in Chapter 5. Are these some of your issues? How can giving over control to God truly give you freedom?

16. Make a list of the choices you are making now related to your spiritual life and your eating disorder. Make a comparative list of what choices you need to make daily to find victory in this battle. In the coming days, weeks, and months, journal about the choices you are making and ask God for strength and wisdom to make good choices moment by moment.

Prayer

Dear Heavenly Father,

Lift the veil from my eyes so that I can see the truth clearly about my disorder, what my life has become because of it, and the sin that I am in. Help me to submerge myself in You and to know that through You I am not powerless against the enemy. Help me to be on my knees in prayer, to open my heart to understand how Your Word is the light unto my path, and to relinquish those control factors that give Satan a foothold in my life. Amen.

CHAPTER 12

His Masterpiece, His Child

*"How absurd it must seem to God when His creatures look to
one another to determine their value. God calls His children to
absolutely reject the world's standards of worth. Feelings of both
pride and inferiority are lies because our worth has nothing to do
with other people. Instead we should value ourselves and others
based on unchangeable spiritual truths. All humans are both made
by God and loved by Him."*
– Julianna Slattery[1]

By March of 2005, I had learned to rely on God's strength
more and more with each new day. As I submerged
myself in God's Word and remained at His feet, little by little,
He began to reveal to me issues that had waged war on my soul
and kept me dependent on my eating disorder. Issues of love,
acceptance, perfectionism, fear of failure, self-image, and control
that I still needed to face. Years ago when I battled my eating
disorder, I never faced those issues head-on. I had learned to deal
only with the loss of my friends. The Lord definitely used that
time to grow me up, but now He was bringing those difficult
issues to the surface, as well as revealing to me the deeper issues
of trusting in His faithfulness, faith in His purpose and plan,
and finding my worth in Him.

God, the Artist and Master Craftsman

I continued to struggle with the Psalm 139 verses. It was apparent that I did not see myself as worthy and lovable. The choice to begin controlling my weight when I was thirteen wasn't just because of the loss of my friends. It was also because of the view I had of myself. If I could control my weight, then I could find my value in that. I could feel good about something I did, in the way I looked, and how others viewed and accepted me. I strived for that perfection in my life.

God was starting to churn up issues in my heart and teach me about my significance as His creation. He kept drawing me back to Psalm 139. In fact, I would get angry every time I read it somewhere or someone else read it to me. At some point I recognized that God wanted me to look at it more closely, to see the truth within the words: "*You* created my inmost being; *You* knit me together in my mother's womb." Had I not seen the significance in that before? It is amazing to think that I am a creation of the holy and living God, made perfectly by *His* hands, uniquely designed and intricately crafted by the God of the Universe. I knew this in my head, but had I ever really thought about its value? The remainder of that verse says, "I praise you because I am fearfully and wonderfully made." Did I believe that? Did I believe in my heart that I was truly fearfully and wonderfully made? Could I say without doubt that I believed the Bible to be true, and then not have it penetrate my heart, affect my life, or change the view I had of myself? I was made with God's hands. He crafted me. I knew that He was perfect, but were His creations perfectly made? I began to question what I believed and the source of how I felt about myself.

Ferguson also writes in his book, *A Heart for God*:

> The universe in which we live is not an accident, not the chance result of "nature" or "evolution." It is the handiwork of the living God. This world in which we live did not just "happen." It was created for a purpose.

... If you read through this chapter (Genesis 1) slowly, you will notice this pattern in the progression of events: God speaks; a new stage of creation takes place; God rejoices in the goodness of what He has made...But then, quite unexpectedly, a new pattern is introduced in Genesis 1:26. God enters into divine council; He determines to make man, not according to His kind, but "in our image, in our likeness;"... Man is patterned on God! He was made to represent God—in created human form."[2]

Yes, I am sinful and imperfect, but only because of the fall, described in Genesis 3, not because of how I was created. In fact, God's creation of me, just like His creation of the universe, was not an accident. I am a handiwork of the living God. His creation of me involved being made in His likeness and image, different from His other creations.

The Bible says:

So God created man in his own image, in the image of God he
created him; male and female he created them and let them rule
over the fish of the sea and the birds of the air, over the livestock,
over all the earth, and over all the creatures that move along the ground.
(Genesis 1: 26-27)

I am patterned after God and made for a purpose, to be His reflection here on earth. What a privilege that is.

We vacationed at the beach at the end of May 2005, about four months after my ER visit. Every morning about 6 A.M. the sun would pierce through our bedroom window and wake me up before anyone else. I decided, the first morning there, I would get up and run before the house started hopping. I went down to the beach. There was only one other person as far as I could see. The sun was rising over the water and the waves were crashing at my feet. It was calming, but strong. I could see, and feel, God's presence in His creations all around me.

As I ran, I started to praise God for His beautiful creations and I recognized His mighty power. I was in awe of who He is as Creator of the Earth. Being at the beach was such a blessing. It helped me to see God as the ultimate artist and craftsman that He is and see His world as an amazing canvas of beauty. I was praising Him for His creations all around me, and then He said, "But, Leigh-Ann, you are one of My beautiful creations, one of My most precious masterpieces. When will you see that and cherish that creation as you cherish these others?" I stopped running and sat down in the sand. I put my face in my hands and cried. The Lord was right. I had not cherished His creation of *me*. In essence, I was saying that I doubted His perfect design and workmanship of me. I thought He had done an amazing job with His other creations, but somehow He had made a mistake when He created me.

Even though I was sitting on a sunny beach, I began to think about snowflakes. Each snowflake that God creates is unique and different. The shape of the snowflake, its intricate design and detail differs from the next. How much time and care God must put into the detail of each one of His falling creations. I started to think about the human race. If God put that much effort into the uniqueness of every snowflake, how much care and design He must put into the creations He has made in the image of Himself. Each one of our bodies and our personalities differ from the next. How beautiful it is that we are all so uniquely made. How could I deny His care and handiwork of me any longer?

I had failed to recognize how special I am because of my uniqueness, which included all the intricate details of my identity that He so carefully designed. I had not seen my worth in that, had not recognized the beauty of His workmanship, and had not seen the value of His masterpiece. This was significant to me and a turning point in seeing the heart of my value. I am His beautiful creation like these others, but I was also fearfully and wonderfully made in His image. And, even beyond that, after God created me He saw that it was good.

Both Sinclair Ferguson in his book *A Heart for God* and Julianna Slattery in her book *Beyond the Masquerade,* were influential in bringing to light for me the fundamental spiritual truths of my worthiness as God's creation, being made in His image, and being created for a purpose. Believing these truths helped me to focus on the source of my significance and worth. God was showing me that my worth, my value and my purpose, rests in the fact that I am His. He is the holy and living God who does not make mistakes. He creates masterpieces; masterpieces that have purpose.

When I was in college I took a class on art history and identification. I have a great appreciation for art. I love to admire the beauty, care, and detail put into each piece and discover what effect it has on me. The extent of my drawing, painting, or creating expertise, however, doesn't go much further than stick figures. So I opted to take a class on identifying pieces of art, understanding the background of each piece, and the learning about the artist who created it. It quickly became one of my favorite classes. I learned that when an artist, sculptor, or craftsman creates a work with his hands, it always has purpose. That purpose may be to tell a story, evoke or express an emotion, or have some practical use, but whatever the purpose of its creation, its beauty, design, and handiwork stem from the depths of its creator.

Great artists are known for the signature aspects of their work. The pieces of themselves that are found in each unique design, so as others view their masterpieces, there is no question as to who the designer or creator is. Claude Monet is known for beginning the impressionist movement. His paintings are clearly an expression of what he saw within a landscape or in nature. Pablo Picasso is known for creating cubism, where he manipulated shapes and colors to show a three dimensional shape on a flat surface. Since the early 1900's, artists have tried to copy these styles in their own works, but authentic paintings by Monet and Picasso are clearly identifiable.

All week, at the beach, I would see God's wonderful creations and masterpieces around me and journaled:

> *May 10, 2005*
> *Dear Heavenly Father, This morning, as I ran, I saw the footprints in the sand of Your creations. Human prints, dog prints, bird prints, and even crabs scurrying along. This evening we made a bonfire on the beach. The stars above lit up the night sky, our toes burrowed through the sand below, the waves beside us crashed like thunder, and the fire at our fingertips warmed our bodies. As I looked at those beautiful creations, I remembered that I was one of them, but made in Your image. I thought about how, because of that, my beauty is dependent upon how much I reflect You. I am special because of Your handiwork and the unique way that You made me.*

A few days into our vacation, my daughter Emily (who was then seven) and I were walking along the beach and talking about beauty. She asked me if she was beautiful. I said, "Yes, absolutely!" As I continued, the Lord gave me the words that I so desperately needed to hear myself. I was shocked that I did not talk about Emily's sparkling blue eyes or her long locks of blonde hair. I did not talk about her long legs and thin body. I did not talk about her sweet dimples or cute little nose. I told her that because she was uniquely designed by God, intricately formed with His hands, and made in His image to reflect His character, she was beautiful.

She said, "Mommy, what does it mean to reflect God's character?" As I explained it to my daughter, it was like Christ was sharing it with me, His daughter. I said, "Emily, since you were made in God's image, the more you learn about Him and His character and the more you become like Him, the more beautiful you are. When you are an example to others of His love and goodness, when others see Christ in you, and your actions glorify God, that is what makes you beautiful. That is what others will see, remember, and want to be like, too."

During that conversation, I was very aware of God's perfect timing. Just a few days before that, my answer to her question would have been full of what the world sees as beauty. The example I had previously set for her with the way I was eating was full of pride, vanity, and control. It was lacking everything that would exemplify Christ and glorify His name.

That evening when I went in to take a shower, I looked at my naked body in the mirror. I looked at myself differently than I ever had before. I looked more intently, thinking about my reflection. I did not pick apart my body, but instead, looked at myself as a masterpiece of the Holy and Living God. I looked at His design, detail and handiwork of me. I was a work in progress. He was whittling away at the part that was of the world, but for the first time I saw His signature aspect. Emerging from within was a woman who was beginning to reflect His character and His heart.

The Purpose of His Masterpiece

When I started to truly see the emerging beauty of God's character in me, and begin to value the fact that I am His masterpiece, I began to recognize how my earthly body had so much worth and beauty simply because I am a believer in Christ. My body, this creation that I had been totally abusing, was also a dwelling place for the Holy Spirit. I read in 1 Corinthians 6:19-20, "Do you not know that your body is a temple of the Holy Spirit, who is in you, whom you have received from God? You are not your own; you were bought at a price. Therefore honor God with your body." I definitely had not been honoring God with my body. In fact, I had been destroying His temple. Romans 12:1-2 came immediately to mind as I had been meditating on the 1 Corinthians Scripture. It says, "Therefore, I urge you brothers, in view of God's mercy, to offer your bodies as living sacrifices, holy and pleasing to God - this is your spiritual act of worship." *My body as a living sacrifice? And how is that my spiritual act of worship?* The Lord reminded me that my body is not my own. He created me for a purpose to house His Spirit and to reflect His character. How special! How incredible! What gift of value! Taking care of His creation, His dwelling place was my spiritual act of worship and a way to honor my Creator, my Lord, and my Savior.

Love and Acceptance From a Father to His Daughter

If I knew my worth was in Christ, if I knew that He loved me as His daughter and His creation, then I had to ask myself why I kept seeking love and acceptance from others. I had put so much value in what other people thought, and I wasn't sure why that was so important to me. I was a people-pleaser and terrified of failure, which fueled my desire for perfection. I think part of my obsession with my outer appearance was that it kept my focus off of my inner appearance—my heart and my vulnerability—which I was terrified to let others see. My whole life had been dominated by fear of rejection and conditional love, and now it was no different. I felt like a failure as a wife, mother, and youth leader because of the limitations of the IC, and I felt that I had failed Emily. Since I was so wrapped up in my own issues, I missed what was going on with her.

My eating disorder had become more aggressive as the feeling of failure had increased in my life, because controlling my weight had been the measure of my success and perfection. I was terrified of what failing meant in my eyes. As I began to see myself as worthy, and recognizing I was a beautiful creation in Christ, the Lord showed me the depth and sufficiency of His great love for me.

Family relationships and the way others treat you in your formative years can have a lasting effect on self-image. A desire for love and acceptance because of a lack of it in childhood is a common thread with those who suffer from eating disorders. Some women have said that they have not been able to fully experience God's love because the view they have of Him was formed by the relationship they had with their earthly fathers. This seems to make sense when we hear from professionals that a majority of women who suffer from eating disorders have had fathers who are absent and critical, fathers who pressure their children for success and perfection, whose love is conditional, or who are emotionally distant in the lives of their daughters. These women hunger for their father's love and acceptance.

Little girls would rather die than fail their daddies. We need and want them to love us unconditionally and be proud of everything we do. For those whose fathers do not, it greatly affects who they become and how they feel about themselves. I agree that our relationship with our Earthly father shapes our view of God, but I will say this: we are all human and we all make mistakes. As a parent, I know that I continually strive to be an example of God to my children, but there are still areas where I fail them. That is human nature. It's not an excuse; it is reality.

The need for love and acceptance may also be the result of how you were treated by other children or siblings when you were growing up. The effect that has on our psyches is huge. Feelings of inadequacy and invalidation that stem from your childhood may still haunt you. Those feelings may not just affect the view you have of yourself, but also affect your relationships with others. However, as I began to recognize and acknowledge the source of my need for acceptance and perfection, I also recognized that I needed to move past that and seek unconditional love through Christ.

159

The reality is that no matter who you or your parents are, what your upbringing or childhood situation was, you will always have a skewed view of God until you come to know Him personally, grow in the knowledge of who He is and apply those spiritual truths to your life. Again, this is why there is a direct correlation between wellness and spiritual growth.

I urge you not to get caught up in the blame game ("I am this way because of the way someone treated me.") I am not minimizing what you have gone through or the hurt you have experienced. Although this need for love and acceptance is real and may stem from a lack of it in your childhood, whether from family members, other children, or significant influences in your life, you need to work through this pain and hurt, no matter how deep it runs, and move into forgiveness.

I do not blame anyone else in my life for the behaviors I have chosen. Restricting food or binging and purging were my choices, not theirs. The things I wish had been done differently I have learned from and choose not to do and teach my children not to do. I also have to remind myself that growth is a process for us all. The determination my husband and I have to be examples of God's love to our children and to encourage them to be that way to each other and to others, will lessen the chance of them growing up feeling poorly about themselves or making others feel poorly about who they are. But, because we are all human and will undoubtedly fall short of God's guidelines, there's no guarantee.

I realize that for some of you the conditional love and lack of acceptance you may have experienced in childhood is more than what I am speaking of. You may have been abused as a child; in which case, I can only say that there is no excuse and I am sorry that you had to experience that. There is more hurt and pain that you need to work through to come to a place of forgiveness. If you are not already in counseling, I strongly urge that you go. The truth is, though, no matter what your experience, abuse or not, you may never receive the kind of unconditional love that you are looking for from man. You may never hear the words "I am sorry" or "I am proud of you" or "You are a beautiful person" from the ones you want to hear it from the most. However, to know that God's love is sufficient, and with that, you have the power to release yourself from this addiction is tremendously freeing.

When God clearly said to me, "Leigh-Ann, you can be angry with Me, but I will always love you; My love for you is unconditional, unwavering, and all the love you will ever need … that will never change," there was mighty power in that. He was saying, "not only should you find your worth in Me, and only Me, but you should also know that My love and acceptance should be enough. He was right; His love was and is truly sufficient. And wait, I know what you are thinking … "But we are designed for relationship. We yearn for that physical companionship and love from another human being." Yes, God does put people in our lives to be an example of His love, but not to take the place of the value of His love. No love from a human being can compare to the unconditional love of the Father who created me and thinks the world of me. I could finally see the significance of myself as His daughter, His precious child, and His beautiful masterpiece. It wasn't just in my head, but had finally translated into my heart and I was filled with joy, true evidence of His abounding and sufficient love. In fact, His love was more than enough, my cup runneth over.

I knew that no matter what I did, God would always love me and accept me. His Word in Romans 8:35-39 was proof of that:

> Who shall separate us from the love of Christ? Shall trouble or hardship
> or persecution or famine or nakedness or danger or sword? As it is written:
> "For your sake we face death all day long; we are considered as sheep to be slaughtered." No, in all these things we are more than conquerors through him

who loved us. For I am convinced that neither death nor life, neither angels nor
demons, neither the present nor the future, nor any powers, neither height nor
depth nor anything else in all creation, will be able to separate us from the love
of God that is in Christ Jesus our Lord.

Not my sins, not my control issues, not even my fear of failure could separate me from the love of Christ. His love was constant, abundant, and never changing. I could rest in that. I discovered that if God's love and acceptance was the only thing that mattered to me, and I truly knew that was enough, then I would never fear failure or rejection again.

I journaled:

May 12, 2005
Lord, I am in awe to think that You, the Creator of the Universe, loves me unconditionally. I am so thankful that You love me more than I love myself or more than anyone else could love me. I am so thankful that You have taken care of me and protected me when I wouldn't. I am amazed at this wonderful love that You, the God of the Universe, has for me. It is a love so foreign to me and a love I don't understand. Help me to see myself through Your eyes; fallen but restored, broken but healed, sinful but forgiven, worthy because I am Your creation, and beautiful as I begin to reflect more of You.

I started to rely on that love instead of fearing the conditional love of man. I knew that we are fallen beings and we will inevitably disappoint others and be disappointed by those we love. Healing came from this knowledge. The fear of rejection from the love of man that began as a child and plagued me as an adult began to clear its way for the security I had found in my Heavenly Father's unconditional and unfailing love. Now I was truly able to see myself as valuable and lovable as His creation and His daughter. His love was sufficient for me. I was experiencing a love I never had before and finding hope, security, and strength in that. Now, it only mattered to me that others would see Jesus in me and that I would be an example of Him. The view I had of myself as a wife, mother, and youth leader was changing. I no longer saw myself as a failure, but now as a work in progress and as an emerging beauty of His reflection.

A Better Wife

The love that Todd and I shared had grown much deeper and stronger than it had ever been. He was my love, my partner, and my encourager, and I was his, but Todd was not my God. He took care of me, loved me, and led me toward the eyes of Christ, but he was not my Christ. His love for me was unconditional when I failed him, but I knew that there would be times when he would fail me too. God had brought us to a deeper love, a selfless love, an unconditional love, and a love that was based on His example.

Todd has been a great checkpoint for me. He helps me see when my thoughts are irrational, and he continues to remind me every day that I am a beautiful creation made by Christ. He had written a poem for me for Christmas. Now, in the midst of finding my value in Christ, Todd read his poem to me again. He had titled it "Loveleigh Eyes." It is a beautiful description of what he sees behind my eyes, in my heart, in the depths of who I am, of who he fell in love with many years ago, and is still in love with today. It was important to me to remember where Todd found my beauty. He is great at reminding me of the person he wrote about.

I was becoming a woman of integrity again, and as I began to be honest with my husband, healing from my hurt began.

It was important to me to be a godly wife. I knew Todd loved me because of who I was, not what I could do for him, and that meant the world to me. Our relationship became better than ever as together we began to rely on Christ and face the challenges that my health issues raised. We were partners helping each other, but relying on Christ.

A Better Mother

Nourishing my body, finding peace, and trusting in God have made a huge impact on my parenting. As I started to nourish my body, I felt stronger physically. That helped me enormously to handle more calmly what was going on around me. I was more relaxed and not so "on edge."

Working through so many of those difficult issues helped me to become a better mother. I wasn't afraid of failing as a mom anymore. I knew that the Lord would give me wisdom as long as I continued to seek His face. I also wasn't such an angry person anymore. I was at peace within my heart and that is clearly what the children saw. They said things like, "Mommy, you are not always in a bad mood anymore," or "You are so nice now, Mommy." I know I was never intentionally mean to the kids, but my anger, fear, and doubt were what I had been reflecting.

Becoming an example of Christ came to the forefront of my mind. It was always there. I kept questioning my reactions to the kids. Was I being a mom of integrity? Was I sharing with them who God is? And, was I praying for wisdom before I would react or respond to them, or afterward when asking for forgiveness?

The things that had to be sacrificed because of my health problems, like wrestling or dancing with them, became less of an issue for me and I think for them as well. I was able to show my affection in other ways, and our conversations had become deeper, more heartfelt, and Christ-centered. My children began to see me trust, remain steadfast, and seek His face in everything.

I had been so concerned about the lack of physical memories, but now I know the spiritual ones will remain.

A Better Leader

As I continued on my battle, I also realized that the way I led my youth girls began to change. I began to share my experiences, God's faithfulness throughout, and what He had taught me. As a result, the girls began to see more of my heart. They didn't see a leader who was perfect, who had it all together, and someone they couldn't relate to. They saw a picture of reality with all the hurts, struggles, and doubts, as well as hope, strength, and wisdom given by the Lord. It totally changed my relationship with them. They saw my heart and I began to see theirs. I am connected to them in a way that I can't explain. I love them dearly and am so thankful that they are in my life. I wrote:

> *May 20, 2005*
> *Lord, I don't see myself as a failure anymore. I know my life doesn't have to be perfect. I don't have to be perfect. I know that with You and through You I have great purpose. I see a difference in my marriage, a difference in my children, and a difference in my relationship with my youth girls. Help me to remain in You, seeing my worth as Your creation and resting in Your love and acceptance of me.*

My heart was different and the way I viewed myself was different. I didn't look for my worth in anything but in being His beautiful masterpiece, created to reflect His character, a dwelling place of His Spirit, and a daughter of the living God.

Journal Questions

1. Read all of Psalm 139. Do you believe that you are the handiwork of the living God? What is uniquely made about you? Can you see that His hands intricately designed that? Do you believe that you are worthy because you were created by God? Why or why not? Can you see that you are a masterpiece created by the master craftsman?

2. Read Genesis 1:26b and 27. What do these verses say about who you are? What sets you apart? Can you cherish the creation of *you* because you were made in His image? Why or why not?

3. Read 1 Corinthians 6:19 and 20. What does this say about the way you treat your body? Do you believe that you have purpose because you are a follower of Christ? Why or why not? How should you take care of the Lord's dwelling place?

4. Where does your need for love and acceptance stem from? Refer back to questions from Chapters 3, 4, and 6. Have you really grieved about that in your life? How can you move past that pain into forgiveness? Can you truly forgive, even if you never receive what you are looking for? Can you accept that God's love is sufficient? How can this bring you freedom?

5. Can you see yourself, not as a failure, but as a work in progress? Look harder. Do you see an emerging beauty, one that is reflecting His character? What is God whittling away right now?

6. How can you become better at the things in your life to which He has called you by recognizing your worth in Him?

Prayer

Dear Heavenly Father,

Help me to see that my worth is found in You. Help me to know that my significance lies in the creation that You made me to be, that I am made in Your image, and that I am a temple of Your Spirit. Help me to move past the pain from my past, to forgive, and to see that Your love is sufficient for me. Amen.

CHAPTER 13

Eating Like a Normal Person

So whether you eat or drink or whatever you do,
do it all for the glory of God.
1 Corinthians 10:31

"We will never know the joy of true freedom until we understand
we cannot take a single step without his help."
Stormie Omartian[1]

As I was growing closer to the Lord, it was becoming easier to eat meals, but I realized that in the last nineteen years I had never really eaten normally. Either I was bingeing and purging, starving myself, or overeating. Since my life from the time I was nineteen until I was thirty-one was full of happiness, blessings, and perfection in my eyes, my eating disorder was not as much of an issue. I did not feel that great of a need to control. However, I did continue to remain a slave to food addiction.

I wasn't terrified of food, and I didn't have enormous binges and purges, but I did separate myself and eat whatever, and however much, I wanted. If stressful situations arose, I always overate and pretended that it was okay; I deserved it. I couldn't restrict or limit food at all or that threw me back into the anorexic mindset, so I just pretended that food was not a problem and "checked out" emotionally when it was time to eat.

Consequently, I gained weight. I realize now that I wasn't healthy. I was really just staying afloat and heading in the other direction. I think, in my mind, I was trying to prove to myself that I didn't have a problem with food and that I could handle it. Did you notice?—*I* could handle it. I hadn't learned to truly be in God's will with my eating, so I never experienced true freedom from the disorder. That's why when life became difficult, I didn't really know how to cope. Now as I was applying spiritual truths to my life, learning to depend on God for my strength, arming myself with His Word, and becoming consistent in my walk with Him, eating did become easier. I no longer feared food or gaining weight, but I still struggled.

One message that I heard over and over from the time I was thirteen was, "Just eat like a normal person. What's the big deal?" If you are struggling through a recovery right now, I know you are laughing at that statement. Everyone with an eating disorder has heard it from time to time. Those who don't have a problem with eating just don't understand. *There* is *no eating like a normal person. I didn't even know what eating like a normal person meant, anyway.* To allow our bodies to feel hungry before we eat, and then eat only what will satisfy the hunger, is something that Americans do not do. We eat for pleasure, recreation, to cure boredom, and to make us feel better, but we do not primarily eat for the sole purpose of nourishing and taking care of the creation God has made in each of us. How was I to know what normal was if most Americans don't eat *normally* or healthy? The world tells us, "Go ahead, indulge. Eat what makes you feel good. You deserve it." And then at the same time says, "You are only beautiful if you are thin and perfect." These conflicting messages are confusing and make it hard to decipher how to truly eat with the right attitude.

I mentioned earlier that for a long time I had no natural cues to tell me when I was hungry, and since I had made poor food choices for so long I didn't really know what was reasonable. I don't really ever remember a time when I ate normally since this all started when I was only thirteen. For the last nineteen years, my thought process with regard to eating was either too restrictive or too lax. It was hard to find that balance, but I knew I wanted to. My fear was no longer about food, but now of being out of the Lord's will with my eating. I wanted true freedom from this disorder. The Spirit was leading me, but I needed some structure along the way as well.

I sincerely wanted to take care of the creation God had made and nourish the dwelling place of His Spirit so that I could be effective for Him. Caring about *this* creation and *this* dwelling place was the first and most important step. Once my heart was in it, and the prayer was in it, then the structure came easily.

Part of the recovery was to assess how I was eating and what areas were difficult for me. I knew that I needed God for the cues, but also for the amount and for the types of food choices I made. At times, when I would allow myself to eat, something in my brain said, "If you are eating that, then eat a lot; you already messed up anyway!" I had restricted my food so much in the past that when it was okay to eat, I went "hog wild" and overate. Overeating set me back into the mindset of wanting to get rid of the food to alleviate that stuffed feeling or restrict the next day. At times I would cut back on my meals so that I could have more of the dessert that I wanted. This mindset was also not good for me. I was eliminating food that was good for me and over-indulging in the foods that weren't. I needed to learn moderation and balance of both.

The whole restrict/overeat cycle was self-perpetuating. The more I would restrict, the more likely I would be to overeat as my body tried to compensate for the reduction in calories. Yet I repeatedly continued to fall into that pattern. I didn't know moderation. I also had difficulty with snacking. I kept finding myself visiting the cupboard, making poor choices, and eating when I really wasn't hungry, especially after dinner when the kids were in bed. Those times of the day had become my time to "pig out" and eat.

Coming Up with Solutions

When trying to come up with solutions in the areas of eating that continued to give me difficulty, I remembered the many books I had read in the past on eating healthy, body image, and the like, and what I had learned from them. I had tried to use this wisdom before, but always failed because I never coupled it with a prayerful, submissive heart rooted in God's Word and strength. Now, having armed myself against the enemy, walking consistently with God, submitting to His will, and desiring to take care of His creation, I was ready to use this practical information on eating right and nourishing my body.

I knew a little about metabolic rate and caloric intake. I knew that our bodies have a set rate at which we burn calories. This rate is triggered by what and when we eat. When we interfere with that by dieting or depriving ourselves of food, then we throw off our whole system of naturally burning calories we don't need and using calories that we do. When we deprive ourselves of food and nutrients (dieting or restricting), then our body slows its rate of burning calories. Then, when we begin to eat normally, our body gains back the weight originally lost because it is still burning at a slower rate. This is why fad diets do not work or only work for a short time. Eating, restricting, eating, restricting is actually detrimental to your body. As you begin to eat what your body really needs consistently and do not restrict, your metabolism will then self-regulate.

Two concepts that I had previously read about stood out in my mind the most. The idea of eating what you want, and when you want, but in moderation and within God's will was something that sounded so simple, but was really very difficult for me until I started to pray first. Listening to the natural, God-given cues from your body, and responding to what your body tells your brain are the foods it needs (by the cravings you have) was monumental for me. It was as if a light bulb went off when I realized that this is God's way of communicating to me what types of foods and nutrients my body needs. Eating the foods our bodies are hungry for, but in moderation, until you are satisfied, not until you are stuffed, is being obedient and faithful to take care of what God has created.

It is not good to completely deny yourself all snacks and junk food, because there is nothing wrong with enjoying food, but pleasure should not be the primary reason we eat. Those types of foods need to be eaten in moderation and not become a license to binge.

The other concept that was helpful to me was honing in on eating in moderation and eating frequently. Eating six to eight smaller meals each day was a significant lifestyle change. I learned that the portions of my six to eight mini-meals should be fist-size and should consist of a healthy protein and a carbohydrate. The purpose of eating several smaller-portion meals throughout the day is so that your stomach never reaches that overstuffed feeling. The portions are small, but frequent so your body is getting enough calories to sustain its natural metabolic rate. At the same time, you are learning to make good food choices. This way of eating eliminates poor snacking habits because you eat small meals throughout the day instead of grazing on whatever you can grab quickly. This concept is from Bill Phillips' book called *Body for Life*.[2]

There is one part of the Body for Life Program that I do not endorse. That is the author's idea of the "free day"—when you can eat anything you want, no matter how much of it you want, for one day of the week. The rest of the week, you follow the regimen. This, to me, is not learning moderation or obedience to eat within God's will. In fact, I think it promotes harsh restriction coupled with binge eating. And this is exactly what would be detrimental to someone with an eating disorder.

The helpful guidelines from *Body for Life* were useful for me as I learned how to eat in a healthy manner, but they were not something I would need to, want to, nor should follow obsessively. I wanted to be careful that I wasn't following any kind of regimen so strictly that it was feeding the control issue again. I still wanted to be dependent on God for all of it. I found that for me, changing my way of eating to more frequent, smaller portions worked great. I couldn't allow myself to get that famished feeling because I would have the tendency to overeat. I needed to eat smaller portions so that I didn't feel stuffed either.

I used a lunch-size plate to portion out my food (I never counted calories or measured out my food in cups) and ate a small, but balanced breakfast; a healthy balanced snack; a small, but healthy lunch; another healthy snack; a well-balanced full dinner on a dinner plate with my family; and then, if I was hungry later, an evening snack. I ate a healthy low-fat protein to build muscles and one or two carbohydrates for energy at each sitting. If I happened to have dessert, then I ate it in moderation. I did not fret about it, nor did I cut out any of my mini-meals. The meals I ate were portioned out appropriately so that I was getting enough calories, and the snacks were healthy choices so that I would feel good about what I was eating. Here's what a typical menu looks like for me:

Breakfast - Low fat yogurt with fresh fruit, sometimes with granola or oatmeal made with skim or 1 percent milk; or an egg and half of a bagel.

Snack - Fresh fruit with low fat cottage cheese or a fruit smoothie, if I did not have fruit and yogurt for breakfast.

Fruit Smoothie Recipe
1 cup of milk, 1 cup of ice, fresh fruit of your choice (I use blueberries, but bananas and strawberries are yummy, too), 1 egg white (for protein); or, you can substitute yogurt for milk, and fresh fruit and ice, or frozen fruit.

Lunch - Turkey, tuna, or chicken whole wheat wrap with lettuce (add mustard if a condiment is needed), or grilled chicken salad with no dressing because of my IC; or a chicken and cheese quesadilla.

Snack - Carrot sticks, cheese and crackers, or a protein bar.

Dinner - Grilled chicken, green beans or a side salad, a roll, and rice or potato.

Evening snack - Fresh fruit or veggies, raisins, or a fruit bar.

Remember, I do not measure out my food or count calories. I just portion them out appropriately by using smaller plates for the mini-meals and a dinner plate only for dinner.

Dessert - I may have dessert occasionally, but I eat it in moderation. Even wise choices can be made in choosing desserts, like having fruit and yogurt parfaits and gelatin instead of pudding; oatmeal cookies instead of peanut butter chocolate chip cookies; or carrot cake instead of chocolate cake (I am not fond of icing, so I scrape that off and enjoy just the cake). Choose fruit pies instead of other types, and eat without whipped cream or with low fat whipped cream or frozen yogurt, instead of ice cream. A friend of mine introduced me to frozen yogurt pies, which I love, and they are good for you.

Another reminder that these are foods I like to eat and can eat because of my IC. It is important that you make healthy choices, but with foods that you enjoy eating. You will not be successful in finding freedom if your choices are not about you and nourishing the creation God has made in you.

I rejected the idea of "forbidden foods" and no longer relied on my "safe foods." I continued to pray to recognize the cues that God was giving me to know what to eat and when to stop. It started to become clear what my body was craving and how much I needed. I knew if I was over-eating or under-eating, and I knew if I was really hungry or just wanting food because of some other reason. My heart's desire had become about following God's will for nourishing my body correctly. Basically, I had to *trust* in Him!

Setting Myself Up for Success Instead of Failure

Part of making good food choices was to have the right kinds of foods on hand. I made a list of foods that I liked, and I filled my cupboards and refrigerator with foods that were good choices with plenty of variety for whatever my body was craving. I started to choose to eat things like smoothies, frozen or fresh fruit like blueberries or melon, yogurt, cheese, protein bars, fruit bars or granola bars, cheese and crackers, salads, fresh veggies, and turkey, tuna, or chicken sandwiches or wraps. Being wise with my food choices was the key to my success. I felt good about what I was eating and wasn't afraid to eat. It also helped to make overeating not an issue. I felt more satisfied after eating several healthy items rather than eating a large amount of junk food, which made me feel stuffed and icky.

I didn't restrict. If I wanted to eat something sweet, I just prayed for help with moderation. I knew if I didn't rely on God for cues, moderation, and strength, it would lead to self-destruction down the road. I also knew that if I prayed, but didn't listen to the cues that God was giving me, then I was openly choosing to sin. I have experienced that when *I* am in control, it is disastrous, so I continue to lay it all at His feet. I trust and know that God will show me. Part of His showing me was my bodily hunger. I started to feel tmy stomach growling and really know when it was time to eat. Sometimes my conscience shows me what my body wants and needs to satisfy my desire and my hunger.

There are times, though, when the enemy has tried to take advantage of my weakness. There are times when life gets hectic or stressful, and I don't always *feel* hungry or I am not recognizing those God-given cues. I don't feel like eating because I am busy, stressed, or not recognizing the need to nourish my body. Be careful of these times. They will appear. Satan uses the slightest manipulation or distraction to get us to fall back into the sin we used to find so comforting. It is during those times when I must reject the feeling of not being hungry, act in obedience, and do what I know is honorable to God.

I could tell when I was in His will with my eating. I was **relaxed,** but not disconnected and overeating. I was eating **healthy,** but not restrictive. Then after a couple of months, I noticed how much easier eating had become, and that I was eating within His will more subconsciously. I was eating normally and I was completely comfortable with that balance. I found more foods that I could eat even with my Interstitial Cystitis, and I truly enjoyed them. It wasn't a chore, a fear, a bad habit, or something that made me hurt. Within His will, it was, as God intended it to be, a necessity for my life, but a pleasure for my lips.

Since I have begun to eat like this, and pray for wisdom, I have realized that my weight really has been easy to maintain because I am eating more consistently, and I am not shocking my metabolism. I am not overeating. I am not starving myself. I am not restricting foods that I enjoy. I still eat yummy foods like cake, pie, ice cream, candy, and my favorite—*cookies*—but in moderation and making wise choices of what kind I select.

I can eat socially on dates with my husband and with friends at parties or restaurants by making good food choices. I don't need to clean my plate, but recognize when I am satisfied, and I can take the rest home for another time. I can choose to have dessert, but be wise about what I order or take from the dessert tray and eat it in moderation. My weight has been the most stable and normal it has ever been. I no longer fear eating. I no longer fear exercising. I care about nourishing my body and being within His will. I just trust that God will work it out for me and He has. There are days that I still fail. It is natural for me to want to control that area of my life. But the days I am out of the Lord's will with my eating, I don't beat myself up.

I know that God is forgiving and He always shows me grace, but then I quickly return to Him for the strength I need and to focus on making right choices.

Some eating disorders recovery programs suggest eliminating from your diet problematic trigger foods, or foods that are binged on, and eating only three full meals a day. They recommend counting calories and points, or never snacking and never having sweets. This type of "recovery" is not finding true freedom from eating disorders. It is what I call only *managing* the disorder. It is not based on obedience to Christ and strength from Him. Who then is still in control? And how long will it really last? Eating like that promotes restrictions and isolates you from others. I think God wants our main priority to be nourishing His creation by making healthy choices, but I don't believe that He wants us to miss out on foods that we enjoy. If that were the case, then He would not have given us taste buds!

God wants you to experience the pleasure of His food. He wants you to be able to eat in social settings, at restaurants, at parties, or with others who have prepared a meal. The priority should be to nourish your body first, making good choices about that, but also to enjoy the foods that He has created. This is about finding freedom and learning to trust God, not about more restrictions, control, and isolation.

Through this whole experience, the Lord was teaching me to trust Him. I realized that the more I knew about God and His character, the easier it was to trust Him. God has never failed anyone. That is evident in His Word. He is always faithful and trustworthy. So I knew that there should be no fear in trusting God with my weight and relinquishing my control to Him.

I know He loves me more than anyone else loves me. He created my body and wants me to nourish it, so I am okay with whatever weight appears on the scale. I know that as long as I am continually following Him, I am not going to be unhealthy. I was able to see that there were times when it didn't even feel like food was an issue and then other times when I knew I needed to be on my knees. I know it is just what God uses to keep me dependent on, and trusting in, Him. I know I will always need to keep that at the forefront of my mind. There is freedom from the sin, but also an awareness of my dependency in Christ.

One evening in June 2005, I just kept thinking that it really is possible to have true freedom from this disorder. At one time, though, I thought I would always be enslaved to food. I thought I would **never** find balance and freedom in this area. I knew that the Lord gives us what we need in every situation so that we are no longer slaves to sin. I knew God was calling me to dependence and obedience, but I had never seen that as the way to find balance and freedom in my disorder. I wrote in my journal again:

June 18, 2005
Lord, thank You for giving me the answers I need. Thank You for helping me find the way to eat within Your will. I feel so free. I can't even put into words how I feel. . . . Like I was just handed the keys to unlock my prison door! Now that I have been trusting You to guide me, listening for Your voice, hearing it clearly, and obeying Your call, it has become so natural for me to eat in a way that I know is pleasing to You. I no longer think that I will always be an anorexic and bulimic. I don't label myself that way. I know that I will always need You for strength in this area, but I will no longer feel a slave to the sin. I have truly found freedom through You.

Taking Care of the Temple of the Lord

In addition to making good food choices and caring for my body's nutritional needs, it also became clear that I needed to form good habits of nourishing my whole self. That meant regular prayer and quiet times as well as regular, but not, excessive exercise. I now begin my day with prayer and devotions when I wake up, a small amount of exercise, and then a healthy breakfast.

It's amazing how focus and direction at the beginning of my day changes the climate of my whole day. This also helps me to stay diligent in journaling how I feel, instead of *acting* on how I feel—an important key in finding, and maintaining, freedom.

Surviving the Holidays

My first holiday season after I began true recovery, I realized that for anyone, whether someone with an eating disorder or not, the holidays have become a license to binge and indulge in any way shape or form. I heard things like, "I can't wait to eat and eat and eat all that great food on Thanksgiving" and "What I love most about Christmas is that it's acceptable to eat all the food that you want and no one cares because we are all doing the same thing." In fact, when a friend or family member brings something they have made, it is almost offensive to pass it up. There is an overwhelming amount of good food right at your fingertips, sometimes for days on end.

I decided that I needed to have perspective going into the holiday season so that I could remain successful with my eating. My kids and I still baked an outrageous amount of cookies to take to parties and have during the season. We still prepared or partook in large, lavish meals with friends and family. However, what made it different for me this year and what helped me to be successful was to go into it with the knowledge that I first needed to be on my knees for strength. I knew that the holidays had always caused me anxiety with food in the past and I needed God's strength. When I sat down to a meal, I prayed about moderation. I chose to take a very small portion of all the things that were in front of me so I could enjoy what others had prepared. However, I recognized that since there was a bigger selection of food to eat, the size of my helpings needed to be significantly smaller than what I would normally take. I still filled up my dinner plate, but with more variety of food and smaller portions.

After finishing the food on my plate, I wanted more. This food was really good and I enjoyed eating it, but then I had to ask myself if I was truly hungry for more or if I just wanted more. I was *not* hungry. In fact, my stomach was filled, but how could I deny eating any more of that savory food? Then I got it. I politely asked my family if they had any objection to me making a plate for later. Of course they all said, "No, help yourself." So instead of a second helping I didn't need, I made a plate of all the foods I really wanted another taste of. It made for a wonderful dinner the next day.

Likewise, desserts can be a downfall, too. I again prayed for wisdom and strength to eat them in moderation and wrapped some up for later. Get-togethers in my home were perfect. I made little plates of a variety of desserts for others to take home when they left for the night so I wouldn't have all the leftovers of things I knew would be difficult for me to resist. Again, making good food choices and using God's strength to eat in moderation is the best defense in surviving the holiday binge-fests.

Helpful Hints

- Journal your thoughts and feelings before and after eating.
- Use God's word to combat irrational thoughts, feelings, and lies from the enemy.
- Pray for strength and wisdom in eating. Pray continually and then at each crossroad with food. Pray to know what, when, and how much to eat. Pray for forgiveness when you fail, and do not beat yourself up, but return quickly to the Lord who provides you with strength and grace.

- Rest in God's power and sufficiency.
- Relinquish control factors and rid yourself of anything that aids the enemy (scales, obsessive exercise, and full-length mirrors if need be; anything that keeps you in control and gives Satan a foothold).
- Eat smaller, well-balanced, more frequent meals to maintain the nutrients needed, stabilize your metabolic rate, and prevent that overstuffed feeling.
- Have a prayer and accountability partner: a friend, a spouse, a parent, or a counselor who can pray on your behalf and monitor your progress until you can do this on your own.

Journal Questions

1. How long has it been since you have eaten like a "normal person?" Can you pinpoint when you could no longer look at food as others do?

2. Can you honestly say you *want* to eat within the Lord's will? Is your heart in it? Are you praying and journaling consistently?

3. Assess how you are eating. What areas are difficult for you? Can you see a pattern that you have fallen into?

4. What areas do you need to address?

5. What healthy steps do you need to take to eliminate them as problem areas?

6. Can you ever see eating as pleasurable, without fear, without restrictions, without rituals?

7. In what areas are you failing to trust God ?

8. Do you believe that you can be free from this disorder? Why or why not?

9. How can dependence and obedience bring you freedom?

10. What keys do you need to have to unlock your prison door?

Prayer

Dear Heavenly Father,

Help me to see the areas of abnormal eating that I need to address. Help me to come up with solutions to eat in a way that is pleasing to You. I want to be able to enjoy eating again. Help me to develop the keys, or answers, I need to unlock my prison door. Help me to depend on You for strength and obey You even when it is hard. Lord, forgive me when I fail and fall to temptation, and help me to quickly return to You. Amen.

CHAPTER 14

Don't Look at the Mountain

*"Why is it so important that you are with God, and God alone, on
the mountaintop? It's important because it's the place in which you
can listen to the voice of the one who calls you the beloved."*
– Henri Nouwen[1]

As the Lord was working in me, changing my heart, and
as I learned to rely on Him, my feelings of anger that
had been so overwhelming just seemed to dissipate. I wasn't
angry at God anymore. I was thankful for His strength and I
was learning to live with my daily pain.

In July of 2005, Todd and I discovered that we were
expecting our third child. We were shocked, surprised, excited,
and scared all at once. We had always wanted a third child, and
even had a girl's name picked out that we were hoping to be able
to use one day, but we weren't really trying to get pregnant at
that point. We were also a bit scared because of my recent bout
with anorexia and we were unsure of how a pregnancy would
affect my health issues.

As the baby grew in size, becoming more active and putting
pressure on my bladder, the pain began to increase. Because
of my Levator Ani Syndrome, as my pelvic muscles began to
soften to make way for delivery, I could no longer hold myself
in alignment. These two circumstances made my daily pain
unbearable. By the time I was four months pregnant, I could no

185

longer walk on my own. I needed assistance, or I would crawl. On my good days, I could lean on the walls to get around the house. Some days the pain was so great, I honestly did not know how I was going to live through it. More times than not, I cried or was curled up in agony.

At five and a half months, I started going to physical therapy. Each week my physical therapist would put me back into alignment and do strengthening exercises for my IC and my Levator Ani muscle. I continued with these exercises at home. The therapy was helping the muscular problem tremendously and I was able to walk again on my own almost immediately. However, the pain from the pressure of the baby on my bladder continued to increase for the duration of the pregnancy. The day after I started physical therapy, I was placed on bed rest for complications with my unborn child, separate from my own health issues. The baby was small and the amniotic fluid was extremely low. The concern was that if the fluid is low, then the umbilical cord is not free flowing and could easily wrap around the baby's neck. Since the baby was small in size, it could also mean that there was not enough oxygen for healthy growth. *Slam!* Blind-sided by the blow of more pain and more reality that I cannot always protect my child from harm.

Thankfully, during this time the Lord provided us with lots of help from family, church members, and friends for cooking, cleaning, and caring for the children. We look back now and see how blessed we were that God provided for our every need. For six weeks of my bed rest, Todd was laid off of work. What a gift from God to have him home to care for me during that time. God even made sure that we were not strained financially while he was off work.

While I had not been walking on my own and was on bed rest, there was no opportunity to exercise. I was almost completely sedentary. Since I was not exercising, I was gaining more weight than I wanted, and the enemy tried to tempt me again with food issues. I kept hearing in my head, *Leigh-Ann, you are not in control of your weight. You are not in control of anything that is happening to you, or your baby, and just what are you going to do with that?* Because of my unbearable pain, my complete dependence on other people, my overwhelming worry for my unborn child, and my significant weakness against this temptation, I felt like I was up against this huge insurmountable mountain that I knew I couldn't climb on my own.

Again, I started to get angry. I started to get scared, and I thought about running. Those emotions tried to creep back in as I felt completely out of control. Yet again God said, "Leigh-Ann, do you *trust* Me? Do you *really trust* Me?" So, instead of how I typically responded to hardship, now when the pain was unbearable, when I felt weak against the enemy, and when my worry was overwhelming, I would close my eyes and envision my Father in Heaven on His throne. I would picture myself crawling up into His lap as He wrapped His arms around me. I could hear His voice speaking to me, "My child, don't look at your mountain. Look at Me. Remember, *I* am all the comfort you need in your pain. I am all the strength you need to remain strong with this food addiction, and I am all the peace you need to know that at this very moment My hands are molding and making your unborn child. Everything that is happening is all within my allowable will for this baby. Just as I have a plan for your life, I also have a plan for this child's life."

I was obviously concerned about my child, and didn't want anything to happen. But I was able to rest, knowing that even if my baby didn't live, or lived and had problems, or lived and was fine, but faced his or her own trials later in life, I knew that my Lord is faithful and would be sufficient for my child just as He was for me.

God's words gave me such peace. I came across the Scripture again that I had originally had such a hard time with, the one God had used to show me my worth in Him as His creation, fearfully and wonderfully made. But now it was speaking to me in a new way. It was speaking to me in a way that didn't have to do with my own creation, but the creation of my unborn child. God's hand was in it all. Now I could claim these words for my baby:

> *For you created my inmost being; you knit me together in my mother's womb. I praise you because I am fearfully and wonderfully made; your works are wonderful, I know that full well. My frame was not hidden from you when I was made in the secret place. When I was woven together in the depths of the earth, your eyes saw my unformed body. All the days ordained for me were written in your book before one of them came to be. (Psalm 139:13-16)*

Todd wrote in his journal:

> *February 26, 2006*
> *I was so excited to find out that we were pregnant again, but I was worried about how all this would affect Leigh-Ann. I didn't think she would revert back to the anorexia. I know she cares more about our child inside than the eating disorder. She is stronger now. I feel so upset when she is hurting. I get a sick feeling in my stomach. I want to take the pain away. I try to take care of her, try to make it better for her, and make her as comfortable as I can. I hate what she is going through. I know it is bringing her closer to You, God. She tells me that and I know she is a different person now, but it is still hard to watch her hurting. I feel like we have been lucky to have had two healthy pregnancies and two healthy children. I question if we will be lucky enough to have a third. I am scared of what may happen. The doctors seem concerned, but I know God, You are taking care of us all.*

On March 28, 2006, I was scheduled to have a C-section. We got up early that morning and as I was getting ready I went into labor on my own. By the time we got to the hospital and prepped for surgery, the resident doctor asked if I wanted to try to deliver vaginally. I had had two previous C-sections, and with my pelvic floor problems, I wasn't sure I would be able to, so I declined and went ahead with the surgery. When the doctors began to pull the baby out, I heard, "Hurry, we've got cord here!"

Because of the low amniotic fluid, the cord had wrapped around the baby's neck three times and was tangled. Quickly, the doctor cut the cord, and then we heard crying. We were so relieved. Our baby girl, Annaleigh Alayna, was born healthy, perfect, and weighing in at 6 pounds, 9 ounces.

The moment I saw my baby's face was the most amazing moment. I looked at her and saw such a picture of God's faithfulness in our lives. It was not because she was okay, but because of where God had taken us. He had carried us up our insurmountable mountain and, at that moment, was rejoicing with us at the top.

The next morning when the doctor came in to check on us, he said, "You made the right decision for the C-section. If you would have tried to deliver her vaginally she may have died because of the pressure of the cord around her neck." God's protective hand was truly on us and I could see His purpose for it all; to learn to depend on His strength and to trust in His faithfulness. This had been the first time in my life that when I was faced with something difficult, I did not fall into the temptation of wanting control and use food as a coping mechanism. I had finally learned how to rely on Christ and trust in His plan, and I came out stronger. I had truly found my freedom.

Journal Questions

1. What would it take for you to look at Christ instead of at your circumstances? How can you do that?

2. Do you believe God is the comfort you need in your pain? Are you experiencing His comfort? Why or why not?

3. Do you believe that God's strength is all you need to fight the temptation of the enemy? Are you using His strength to fight? Why or why not?

4. Do you believe that God's peace is overflowing? Do you feel that peace on a daily basis? Why or why not?

5. Do you believe that God has given you all that you need to make it through your difficult situations and come out stronger? Why or why not?

6. If you are not experiencing God's comfort, strength, and peace, can you see that it is because of a choice you are making? God is reaching out to meet you right where you are to pull you up to safety. How can you let go of your circumstances, reach out to Him, let Him take hold so that you can begin to experience Him at work in your life?

Prayer

Dear Heavenly Father,
Help me to see that Your comfort, strength, peace, and love are sufficient for whatever I face . As I work through the pain in my life, help me to always seek Your face, reach out for Your hand, and allow You to work. Amen.

CHAPTER 15

Pain Has Purpose

"He will sit as a refiner and purifier of silver" (Malachi 3:3).

I continued to struggle with pain, and even though I wasn't angry anymore, I kept asking God, "Why?" Why so much pain? Then I recognized a pattern in my life. God kept using pain to get my attention. Whether my pain was emotional or physical made no difference. So, there must be some purpose to this pain. It was necessary, even vital, in my life. As awful as it is to live with pain, as much resistance as I have for it, living without it would be horrific.

Unfortunately, there are people who live without the ability to perceive pain. Philip Yancey, in his book, *Where Is God When it Hurts?*, discusses in the chapter entitled "Painless Hell," individuals who no longer feel pain due to leprosy or a rare condition known as Congenital Indifference to Pain. Patients with CIPA were born with the absence of the small nerve fibers that carry the sensation of pain from the nerve ending to the brain. Therefore, they can, and do, get hurt, but they just don't feel it. In fact, they can feel other sensations like a tickle or an itch, but they cannot feel pain or differentiate between hot and cold.

There are countless cases of deadly wounds, infections, broken bones, burns, and injuries that may even be self-inflicted because of the absence of the warning sign that alerts people's body to harm. I never thought I would say this, but I'm thankful that I feel pain. I'm thankful for its purpose in my life both physically and spiritually.

Pain has purpose—to change our hearts, transform our minds, and mold us into His likeness.

When I read the following story it impacted me significantly and helped me to understand that the pain God allows in our lives is for a very loving and beautiful reason.

"He will sit as a refiner and purifier of silver" (Malachi 3:3). This verse puzzled a woman about the character and nature of God. She went to watch a silversmith at work. He held a piece of silver over the fire and let it heat up. He explained that in the refining process one needed to hold the silver in the middle of the fire where the flames were the hottest to burn away all the impurities. She asked the silversmith if it was true that he had to sit there in front of the fire the whole time the silver was being refined. He answered, "Yes, because I must keep my eyes on the silver. If it is left a moment too long in the flames it will be destroyed." The woman asked, "How do you know when it is fully refined?" He smiled at her and answered, "When I see my image in it."[2]

The moment of Annaleigh's birth changed my life in a huge way. It changed the way I viewed the hardships God allows in my life. Now when I am faced with a trial, I immediately go to my knees and say, "Lord, this pain that you have allowed ... I know it is for a purpose and I will trust that it is part of Your plan in my life. Give me Your strength to endure." I seek to find the joy in the suffering and how God may be using it to bring me closer to Him. I can see how pain can truly be a blessing as it burns away my impurities.

Those difficult times in our lives *are* painful. They do hurt, and no one likes to hurt. If you did, then I would wonder about you. Even the word *pain* makes me want to cringe. I would not choose to be in pain. It is hard and many times I feel broken, at the end of myself, and that I want to give up. Everything in me wants to avoid pain, but I know that because we live in a fallen world and because God allows pain for a reason, that it ultimately is unavoidable. I am not minimizing how painful it feels to go through something difficult, how lonely it feels to be wandering in the wilderness, or how cold and scary it is to be stuck in the storm, but I have realized that those times are intentional and purposeful on God's part. He allows them in our lives so that we recognize our dependence on Him, so we seek comfort in Him, so we can become more like Him, and so we can share with others His goodness and grace in the midst of it. Be aware, though, that in those same difficult times Satan tempts, taunts, and attempts to pull us away from God, so we become ineffective for Him. He wants us stuck among our anger, fear, pain, and loneliness.

Initially, when I was first diagnosed with my health conditions I had prayed and prayed for healing. I kept banking on the fact that at some point God would deliver me from all this pain, and I was angry when it didn't happen. I had to come to a point with my pain, and with my eating, that maybe it wasn't in God's plan to rescue me from all of it. I had to accept that my pain might be life-long, which meant my dependency would be too. I had to recognize that God is not in the business of making me happy, but in bringing me to growth and true joy, which is only found in Him. Sometimes that means removing things in my life that are stumbling blocks and for me to discover that joy is found when I must depend on Him. I knew that I had chosen to eat the way I had for the last nineteen years, but I also knew that this might, too, be a lifelong dependency. I am unable to get through my day in pain and eating healthy unless I am continually on my knees praying for strength and unless I have a heart that desires to do His will.

These two areas had truly become the thorns in my flesh. The Apostle Paul wrote about the thorn in his flesh in 2 Corinthians 12:7-10:

> *There was given me a thorn in my flesh, a messenger of Satan, to torment me. Three times I pleaded with the Lord to take it away from me. But he said to me, "My grace is sufficient for you, for my power is made perfect in weakness."… That is why, for Christ's sake, I delight in weaknesses, in insults, in hardships, in persecutions, in difficulties. For when I am weak, then I am strong.*

When I am weak, recognizing my need for God, my desire for Him to work in my life, and asking Him for help, then I am really strong.

One thing I realized through this whole process was that my plan for an easy life isn't dependent upon how much faith I have. God will carry out His plan for me no matter what that looks like because of His great love for me and no amount of prayer can change what He has in store for me. The purpose of prayer is not to change God's mind about something He has allowed in my life. The purpose is to change my heart to accept it and to develop a trust in His plan, even when I do not understand it or think that this is not the life I expected. I was starting to get it—all of this pain was changing me, transforming me, and molding me into His likeness.

While we had been vacationing at the beach, my son Christopher walked out onto the deck with no shoes on. I heard a big cry and turned to see him holding his foot. There was a massive splinter imbedded deep within the skin. We scooped him up and laid him flat on his belly on the kitchen table. Todd grabbed some tweezers and a needle and began to work at removing it while I poured hydrogen peroxide on it to wash away the dirt. Christopher was screaming and crying, "Daddy, don't do that. It hurts me. Please stop!"

I explained to Christopher that Daddy had to get it out or his whole foot would get infected. He was squirming and wiggling. I said, "Honey, don't fight Daddy. He is trying to

194

make it better." A lump welled up in my throat, and I had to fight back the tears. It was hard to get those words out. I thought about the Lord. What a true picture of the last years of my life. I fought Him so much with my fear and anger, instead of realizing that He was trying to make me better. He was refining me and washing away my impurities. What a beautiful picture of His love for me. He allows the pain that will eventually bring healing and strength. Pain and hardship are inevitable. We live in a fallen world. We allowed the pain in my son's foot so we could remove the dirty splinter. If we hadn't, it would have caused an infection and that would have been neglectful. God's refining, removal of the dirty splinters, is out of His abundant and overwhelming love for us, and that is *beautiful*.

There is purpose to our suffering and there's hope within God's perfect plan. His intent is never to harm. He is a trustworthy God whose purpose is to make me more like Him. I had to stop living on my own terms, for my own will, and then I began to see how this was growing me up. I didn't like the suffering, but I knew that God loved me and there was a purpose for it in my life. He was making significant changes in me that may not have happened any other way. My will and my focus were becoming less about me and more about Christ.

A "Family Circus" comic that made me think of all that was happening in my life was of a little girl who saw a butterfly. She looked up and asked her grandma, "Do caterpillars know they are going to be butterflies or does God just surprise them?" I thought, *How fitting*. Had I known the transformation that God was going to make in my life prior to the pain, would I have resisted Him so much? Would I have been as angry and frightened if I had known why? Maybe not; but then I wouldn't have developed the faith and trust necessary to bring Him glory.

Pain Has Purpose … to Bring God Glory

Those difficult times in our lives are not meant to be easy. If they were, then we could get through them on our own. They are meant to be difficult to bring us to our knees and to recognize that it is His faithfulness that carries us through so that He is given full glory. I know now that I had misunderstood God's promise that He will never give someone more than they can handle. God doesn't say, "I promise I will never give you more than you can handle on your own." He says, "I promise I will never give you more than you can handle with and through Me."

On my own, my mountains (the circumstances in my life that seem so overwhelming) are insurmountable, so instead I fix my eyes on Him. Without a doubt, I can do, and get through, all things through Christ who strengthens me.

> *Therefore we do not lose heart. Though outwardly we are wasting away, yet inwardly we are being renewed day by day. For our light and momentary troubles are achieving for us an eternal glory that far outweighs them all. So we fix our eyes not on what is seen, but on what is unseen. For what is seen is temporary, but what is unseen is eternal. (2 Corinthians 4:16-18)*

It's been four years since I was diagnosed with my health issues. My circumstances haven't changed all that much. I still face my pain daily. I am having surgeries to distend my bladder every couple of months. It is a lot to put my body through. I have had some complications along the way, but the procedures do help. It is temporary help, but better than nothing. So far, though, there is no real medical answer to my health issues and that is frustrating and hard.

Life is like that sometimes. We experience hardships, and this is not what we expect or plan. But our journey can be exciting, comforting, and refreshing when we rest in who God is, His sufficiency for whatever we are faced with, and His faithfulness to carry us up our insurmountable mountains where He rejoices with us at the top.

Physically I continue to have difficult days, but I rest in Him. I have learned how to rely on God to comfort me in my pain. You may not be dealing with a health issue or the loss of a loved one. These, in addition to my issues with self-esteem and need for love and acceptance were the situations in my life that caused me pain and made me want to control. Maybe you have faced rejection or pain from others. Whether the pain you have experienced is emotional or physical, whether it is in the past or in the present, whether your circumstances have changed or not, God can provide the comfort you need and the strength to get you through.

Just a few days ago, I was having a difficult day with pain and spent most of it in tears. I started to get upset with myself and kept thinking, *Leigh-Ann, find the joy in suffering and rest in Him*, but I continued to weep. Not because I felt sorry for myself or because I was angry, but because it *was* painful. I went to my knees in prayer, and the message God gave me was amazing. He said, "Leigh-Ann, it is okay to be where you are. I will meet you and comfort you there." How freeing! I don't need to be somewhere I'm not. It is okay to weep in the midst of the pain. It doesn't feel good. But to know that God will meet me there is incredible and so overwhelmingly loving.

At some point during my last pregnancy, I found myself meditating. Now, I know that conjures up weird thoughts, but let me explain. My meditations were just closing my eyes and imagining Christ. Sometimes I would imagine myself crawling up into His comforting lap and being held by Him. Sometimes it would be His cleansing waters washing over me. Sometimes it would be His healing hand upon the parts of my body that were in pain. Sometimes it was just thinking about who He is. Sometimes it was thinking of His creations, walking barefoot on the beach, and looking at the sunrise over the ocean. These thoughts certainly did not, and do not, remove the pain in my life completely, but they are significantly helpful in easing it. I have found that this comfort, the comfort that comes from Christ is real and lasting and completely sufficient.

My eating disorder was wrapped up in my skewed view that God's protection of me meant I would never face trials or hardships and that life would be fair. If I did face trials or life wasn't fair, He would fix it and make it all better. True healing began when I started to understand who God is. He is mighty and powerful. He is my strength against the enemy. He is merciful and just when I fail. His love is sufficient. He is all-knowing and His plan for me is perfect. He is comforting and He meets me where I am.

God's impact in my life is the gift of His Son. It is that Christ died and rose again to give me freedom from sin, a new life with Him, and eternal salvation, but it is more than that. It is also the gift of His love, His strength, and His peace that I need every day. I know that being a Christian doesn't guarantee that my life will be easy or free from hardships, but it does guarantee that every day as I walk through life, He walks with me. Now, that is where I find my joy and what keeps me away from the cliff. I don't feel like I have to hide my pain anymore or paint the plastic smile on my face. God is glorified when I seek His face, rest in His comfort and strength, trust in His plan for my life, and recognize it is His faithfulness that carries me through.

Pain Has Purpose: God Can Use Us to Help Others

God uses difficult situations to draw his children nearer to Him, to develop a trust and dependency in Him, and to prepare us to be used by Him effectively, glorifying His name and bringing others closer to Him.

> *Praise be to the God the Father of our Lord Jesus Christ, the Father of compassion and the God of all comfort, who comforts us in all our troubles, so that*

we can comfort those in any trouble with the comfort
we ourselves have received from God. For just as
the sufferings of Christ flow over into our lives, so
also through Christ our comfort overflows. If we are
distressed, it is for your comfort and salvation; if we
are comforted, it is for your comfort, which produces in
you patient endurance of the same sufferings we suffer.
And our hope for you is firm, because we know that just
as you share in our sufferings, so also you share in our
comfort. (2 Corinthians 1:3-7)

My comfort is in knowing that He is with me. The comfort
is not in hoping for a physical healing from my IC and Levator
Ani Syndrome, or deliverance from my food addiction, but
in knowing that through all of that God walks with me. He's
strengthening me, and has a purpose for me. His purpose is
to grow me up so that I can be used by Him to further His
kingdom and to help others seek His face in their times of
distress.

While I was at the women's retreat center, Susie gave me a
letter. In it, she said that I was strong, that I persevered, and that
I had a sense that persevering through the pain of today was
hinged on tomorrow's calling. I knew, without a doubt, that
there was a purpose for this pain. I knew as long as I allowed
God to work in my life and had a willing heart, He could use
me for His glory. I journaled:

June 11, 2006
Susie's letter has made me think so much. What is
it you have in store for me, Lord? Just what are You
preparing me for? I know that this life-long dependency
on You for strength and comfort is to be used for Your
glory. My desire to be used by You is strong. Again this
morning when I woke up, the first thing I was aware
of was pain. I hurt so much it woke me out of my sleep.

Instead of being angry or sad today, I realized how special it was that You had given me something to recognize that my first conscious thought of every day was of my need for You. I love You and am so thankful that You have allowed this trial in my life, that You have allowed Satan to sift me, and I have come out nearer to You. I am truly blessed. I want to eat healthy so that I can be used by You to glorify Your name. I keep thinking of the Scripture from James 1:2-4: "Consider it pure joy, my brothers, whenever you face trials of many kinds, because you know that the testing of your faith develops perseverance. Perseverance must finish its work so that you may be mature and complete, not lacking anything."

God's Truth in Our Lives

God has a plan for each of us. We don't know specifically what that plan entails but we do know these things:

- God desires a relationship with us
- God uses the hardships He allows in our lives to mold and make us into His likeness and bring us nearer to Him
- God calls us to share who He is, our experiences, and His work in our lives with others.

In fact, He demands that we share about Him. The Great Commission says:

Therefore go and make disciples of all nations, baptizing them in the name of the Father and of the son and the Holy Spirit, and teaching them to obey everything I have commanded you. And surely I am with you always, to the very end of the age. (Matthew 28:19-20)

What God is teaching us through our hardships, as He molds us more into His likeness, He wants us to share with others in order to make disciples for Him.

The best way I know to share Christ with others is through our experiences, what we know about Christ from our own lives, or from others' life experiences. It is not just head knowledge, but truly sharing your heart. Have you ever tried to share with someone and quoted Scripture verse after Scripture verse, but never shared out of your own experience about Christ in your life? It just isn't as effective. The Bible is full of stories of people's lives and how God works in them for His purposes. We are living testimonies of Him.

I am sure you can think of people He has used in your life to bring you closer to Him. Those who have struggled similarly, or those who just seemed to say what you needed to hear because they have experienced pain in some form or another. Even if it is not exactly the same pain you've experienced, they have directed you back to the face of Christ. This pain we endure is part of His plan, so we can share with others what God has done in our lives and to use us effectively for His glory to further His kingdom.

I appreciate what Stormie Omartian writes in her book, *Just Enough Light for the Step I'm On*:

His desire is that we become more and more dependent on Him for every step. That's because He wants to take us places we've never been, to heights we can't imagine and in order to do that we have to go through the low valleys, treacherous mountains, rough terrain and narrow paths of life.... God promises to be our guide and show us the way for the next steps to take.... His light does not grow dim or go out. If it appears to it is because we have stepped out of the light of His presence.... Often we find ourselves walking in the dark simply because we are not willing to pay the price for having the light.... He gives us just enough to keep us dependent on Him. In that way He can teach us to take bigger steps of faith in order to prepare for what He is calling us to in the future.... Sometimes what seems like the darkest step we've ever been on comes just before the brightest light we've ever experienced."[1]

When God asks us to join Him in His work and be used by Him, it is a privilege, an honor, the brightest light we could ever imagine, yet possibly, the hardest thing we've ever been called to do. Being vulnerable and sharing and reliving our pain is not particularly a fun experience. It is difficult, but just as God was faithful to provide what we needed as we went through it, He is faithful to provide what we need to share it so His work can be fulfilled and He can be glorified. He promises that in the Great Commission. He tells us that surely He will be with us until the end of the age.

God isn't going to call you to something without having prepared you first. Our whole lives are one preparation after another for something He is calling us to later. The pain, growing us up in the midst of it, and learning to glorify Him through it, are all part of Him equipping us for what He has called us to do. He promises to provide what we need in the midst of the sharing as well, not just in the preparation. Then, He blesses our obedience when we answer His call. Ultimately, joining God in His work by helping others to seek Him in their pain, glorifies Him, and it blesses us.

One Sunday in church the message was about this very thing. How is God leading us to further His kingdom, and are we willing to allow God to use our pain if it will bring Him glory? I thought about that for a long time. I asked myself during the service—am I willing to do whatever He wants, *whatever* He asks of me even if it is sharing my pain and publicly confessing my eating disorder? This would require a great deal of trust on my part to believe that God's plan is perfect and purposeful, and that He is sufficient and faithful to carry me through what He was asking of me and preparing me for. I prayed:

> Lord, I know that You are preparing me for something and taking me somewhere I could only get to by bringing me to the end of myself and making me completely dependent on You for every moment. I have to trust that whatever You are calling me to, You will provide me with what I need. I know You are a faithful and loving God. I love You, Lord, and I want nothing more than to glorify You. My heart is willing. I will obey and follow You because I trust in Your plan and Your faithfulness.

That same day, just moments after the service, I was approached by the head of our women's retreat committee. She said, "Leigh-Ann, I don't know your story, but I have felt confirmation from God that I am supposed to ask you to share your story at our upcoming women's retreat." She then told me that the theme was God's faithfulness. I don't know why I was amazed, but I was.

I shared my story just four months later at our women's retreat, and my faithful God carried me through. I was able to glorify Him in a big way and see others' lives changed because of it. I was floored by the amount of comments from others. The common reaction was, "Thank you for being honest and real."

All of a sudden I got it. My testimony was not like those others that I couldn't stand to hear in the midst of my pain; those testimonies of praising God because of healing, new jobs, long-awaited pregnancies, changed circumstances, fairy tales and happily ever-afters. I was happy for those people whose circumstances God had changed and how He had blessed them in those ways, but it was never applicable to me. It was a message I couldn't hear. I would think about the person God chooses not to heal. The one who continues to live in pain. The one who doesn't get to have the happily ever-after. The one who still has to live with a loss. What about all of *them*?

Now, I know where God is in all of that. He remains steadfast and faithful. I was the one who had doubted. My circumstances weren't changing, but now my testimony was one of continual dependency, learning to praise God through it, seeing His goodness in the midst of it, and knowing that He can and will carry me. I trust that it is all part of His plan. It was difficult to share my story, but truly the brightest light I had ever experienced. My pain had purpose.

When I shared with Todd about what happened at the retreat, he journaled:

> *February 5, 2007*
> *When Leigh-Ann came home from the retreat, we talked about how it went. God, I am so glad that You gave her the courage to do this for You. I know it was difficult. Somehow she turned her pain around into something that could help others and serve You. I am so proud of her and so happy that You have used her this way.*

I looked back on the pain in my life and recognized that there was a bigger picture than just what was affecting me. Returning to the point when I first experienced real pain and anger with God—the loss of my two friends—He revealed something significant to me. God showed me that that was part of His plan for their lives. Here on Earth, I will not have the answers to my questions as to why He chose to take them so early in their lives, but I had to accept that if I trusted in His plan for me, I had to trust in His plan for them and know that it was purposeful. I had to recognize the same for my children. The pain of the situations that they have had already, or have yet to experience is about *their* journey and His plan for *them*.

This I must accept and trust that He loves them more than I do. They are His precious creations too. So, whatever He chooses to place in their lives to grow them up in Him, I must embrace and love them through it.

> *March 13, 2007 I wrote*
> *Today, Lord, I keep thinking about my friends and the journey You had for them. Sometimes I wonder if You took them so early in their lives because You wanted to bring them home to be with You. I imagine them in Your arms, experiencing life without pain, and it brings me so much comfort. In a way it makes me long to be home, too. However, I know that for now, my time is here being used by You and that brings me unbelievable joy. While I am here serving You, Lord, I know I will experience pain. Thank You for your beautiful and abounding love that allows hardships in my life so that I can become more like You. Give me strength when I face them and courage to share them. Amen.*

Journal Questions

1. How is God using the pain in your life to change your heart, transform your mind and mold you into His likeness?

2. What is the thorn in your flesh? How can you depend on God for what you need as you struggle with this in your life?

3. How is God using the pain in your life to bring Him glory?

4. Read 2 Corinthians. 4:16-18. How can you fix your eyes on Christ? List practical steps of doing so.

5. Read 2 Corinthians 1:3-7. How can God use the pain in your life to help or comfort others?

6. Can you see the bigger picture here?

7. Read James 1:2-4. Do you consider it pure joy to face trials? Why or why not? How can you come to the place where you do?

8. How can you eliminate being blind-sided by the blow of a trial or hardship?

Prayer

Dear Heavenly Father,

Help me to see that there is a bigger picture at hand, that the pain of today is hinged on tomorrow's calling. Make me a willing servant to be used by You. Use my pain to change me, refine my heart, and make me like You. Use my pain to bring You glory and to help others in whatever way that appears. Amen.

CHAPTER 16

⎰A Reflection of Him

Make the new reflection of my heart be the true image of you.

I am so thankful and blessed that God has allowed such pain in my life because He has brought me back with a stronger dependence, a greater trust, and a deeper love for Him. It is a love I could have never come to without those situations in my life. I am not sure of all the details in God's plan for me, but I do know that He loves me and His ways are perfect, so as it unfolds I will trust and not be afraid. I wrote in my journal:

> *June 15, 2006*
> *Lord, as You continue to reveal more of Yourself to me, I am flooded with emotion. Grief and sadness as I see my sin clearly, joy as I experience Your great love for me, peace as I learn to trust You with all things and through every circumstance and give over my control to You. I pray that my life will reflect Your character and that my will will always remain in line with Yours.*

It has been four years since I was first diagnosed with Interstitial Cystitis and Levator Ani Syndrome, and three years since my last bout with my eating disorder. That chapter in my life was full of struggles, running away, pain, fear, but also it was a time of reconciliation, dependency, and learning to trust. I am a different person now, changed significantly. When I think back on it all, I am overwhelmed. I wrote:

"Mirror, Mirror is that reflection true?
Oh dear God, how I wish I could see You.

I look at my reflection and repeat the words again,
'You are ugly, you are worthless, you're a failure and full of sin'
All the lies that Satan loves to whisper deep within.

It's almost impossible for anyone to see
The feelings so deeply hidden inside of me.
All my anger, all my sadness, all my pain and all my fears
All the things in my life that fill my heart with tears.

I dare not show the world that miserable reflection
It is so much safer to be the model of perfection.

I cannot accept what I cannot control
So I find I am falling deeper into my hole.
The mountain is too treacherous to climb
But I fear I may be running out of time.

But this time as I begin to fall fall fall
I see Your hand and hear Your voice as You call call call
You provide my shelter in the rain
And promise to comfort in my pain.

Lord lift me up into Your lap and never let me go
Hold my broken body in Your hands oh carefully
so
Do not let my fearful eyes turn away from You
Instead dear Lord let me enjoy the most amazing
view.

As I seek Your face and use Your strength to fight
the battle now
Help me to trust, follow and obey even when I am
not sure how
Transform my mind, restore my soul and mold me
to Your likeness too
Make the new reflection of my heart be the true
image of You."

I was struggling and hating my life. I was starving myself, and that had become more important than my family and my walk with God. I was skeletal and afraid, but still starving myself. I was angry and bitter. Now I am celebrating my life and the creation that God has made in me. I feel so blessed that the Lord has taken me on a journey to bring me closer to Him.

I can honestly say that I am thankful for the health issues in my life. They keep me ever dependent on God's strength for each moment of my day. It keeps me trusting Him with His will for my life. It gives me perspective on what is important, and it is a witness to be used for His glory.

I heard a song sung by Christina Aguilera called "Reflection." Part of the lyrics in that song made me question myself, "Who *is* that girl I see staring back at me? When *will* my reflection show who I am inside? How *will* I show the world what's inside my heart?"[1]

I remember a time when I hated the reflection in the mirror. It was full of anger and fear. I didn't see myself as "fearfully or wonderfully made." I didn't see the purpose for this pain in my life or how any of it would make a difference. Now, the reflection of His creation that I see is so unlike what it once was. I see a woman who God is not yet finished with, but one who has made great strides in her walk with Him. I see a woman standing strong against the enemy because of Christ, and one who learned to persevere through the difficult times by seeking and trusting in Him. I see a woman who values His creation and finds her beauty in Him. I see a woman who wants to honor and serve God with her life and reflect His character so that others may know His goodness. I pray that that is what the world will see when they look at me, and I pray that is what my children will see as well, so they, too, will become a reflection of Him. I can say with the writer of Romans 8:28, "And we know that in all things God works for the good of those who love him, who have been called according to his purpose."

Journal Questions

1.We look at ourselves several times a day. Is it possible to look past our outer selves and focus on the heart?

2. What do you risk by searching your heart?

3. Are you willing to take that risk to begin the transformation of your heart? Why or why not?

Honestly take a look at your heart and answer these questions:
- What do I see in my reflection?
- What do I want to see?
- What does the world see when they look at me?
- What do I want the world to see when they look at me?
- What changes do I need to make in my life to make that happen?

Prayer

Dear Heavenly Father,
I pray that the world will see You when they look at me. I pray that I will become an example of You to others in my life. Help me to become a reflection of You. Amen.

CHAPTER 17

For Parents and Loved Ones: Prevention, Red Flags and How to Help

Since God so loved us, we also ought to love one another.
No one has ever seen God; but if we love one another, God lives in us
and his love is made complete in us.... There is no fear in love.
But perfect love drives out fear.... Dear children, let us not love
with words or tongue but with actions and in truth.
1 John 4:11-12,18; 3:18

As a parent myself, I obviously do not want my children to grow up with poor self-images or poor eating habits. I want each one of them to know that they are beautiful because they are one of God's creations, made in His image and a reflection of Him. Here are several preventative measures that parents can take when raising their children to view themselves in a realistic and biblical way:

Be a good role model. Look at your own view of yourself and your body and how you view others' bodies. Children will mimic what they see and hear. Your behaviors have a huge influence in the lives of your children. If you have a negative outlook on your body or are critical of others' bodies, then your children will pick up on that. They will become focused on what their body looks like and see it as negative as well. If you are positive and realistic about your body, then your children will develop more realistic and positive views of their own bodies.

Do not place a great deal of emphasis or importance on outward beauty and body shape. Instead, talk to your children about the importance of being healthy. Talk about taking care of your body, the creation God has made. Discuss the importance of health issues, eating well-balanced meals, and exercising to be healthy versus dieting to lose weight and to change your body type, or exercising to burn calories and to become thinner. Exercise with your children. Talk about how it makes you feel, not that it is something you have to do because you need to lose weight.

Never cut out food and tell them it is because they are too fat or could get too fat. Remember portion control, not restrictions. Never express to them the idea that you or others would like them more if they were more slender. Do not emphasize the shapes of models in magazines or on TV. Those body types are not representative of the average woman or man. They are unrealistic goals. Do not allow or tolerate teasing or criticism of others.

Try to change the ideas that our society has on body images in your home and in your loved ones' minds. What they see in magazines and on TV can be very persuasive. The view that thin is in, beautiful, and powerful, and that fat is ugly and weak can be quite detrimental to a person who has a rounder, bigger body, and it is certainly not biblical. Talk about how we are uniquely designed by God, made with His hands and in His image, and that we are all equally and uniquely beautiful.

Help your loved ones have strong self-esteem and positive views of themselves. In general, express how they are one of

God's beautiful creations, made in His image, and set for a purpose. Help them to see that their beauty is based on their reflection of Christ and help them to develop an understanding of what that means. Emphasize inward characteristics that are Christ-like and share with them that what makes them attractive.

Be your own reflection of Christ and show your unconditional love for them. Show and tell them how much you love them, value them, and are proud of them, with no strings attached. Allow them to make mistakes and correct them in a positive manner. Do not set unrealistic goals for them and punish them if they do not succeed. Do not expect perfection; only Jesus can succeed in that. Let them be a part of decision-making for their lives and helping to set realistic goals for themselves.

WARNING SIGNS
(Also refer back to Chapter 5)

Warning signs or red flags for parents and loved ones are especially important. If you can recognize some behaviors early on then much can be done before the problem gets out of hand. First of all, do not be naïve. Eating disorders can develop in both males and females of any age, race, or socioeconomic background. Do not dismiss a possible warning sign because you feel your child or loved one would never become involved in an eating disorder.

Here are some specific warning signs:

For Anorexia:
- Loss of a significant amount of weight
- Dieting when already thin
- Fear of food or weight gain
- Talk about being fat when thin
- Feeling cold

- Wearing big, baggy clothes to cover up weight loss
- Loss of menstrual periods
- Preoccupation with food, calories, and fat contents
- Interest in cooking for others, but not joining in on eating
- Fainting, weakness, or exhaustion
- Exercising compulsively
- Depression or anxiety
- Shortness of breath
- Constipation
- Growth of fine body hair on arms, legs, etc.

For Bulimia:
- Eating large amounts of food at one time
- Eating when not physically hungry
- Frequent dieting
- Unable to stop eating
- Weight fluctuations
- Disappearances after meals
- Sores or calluses on hands and fingers
- Hidden food or pills (laxatives, diuretics, etc.)
- Swollen glands, puffy face
- Feelings of weakness and dizziness

How to Help in the Midst of Your Own Feelings

Todd was a huge part of my recovery. I constantly tell him that if it were not for him and the way he responded to me, I would not have recovered as quickly and our marriage might not still be intact. Instead, our marriage has become stronger because of the way he loved me through the process, and I am alive to tell my story. He was such a great example of God through it all and he continues to be today. His encouragement, words of wisdom, desire to seek Christ, and loving accountability were necessary factors in my recovery and the health of our relationship. His feelings during it all were so real. Some of these feelings, I'm sure, you can identify with:

Guilt: Resist walking in the shoes of guilt. Even if your parenting or partnership contributed to the disorder, all you can do now is recognize that and change your point of view for the health of your loved one. Do not beat yourself up for the past. Look at what you can do now in the present to be a source of strength to help your loved one get better. They need to experience your love, your encouragement, and your accountability, not your judgment, fear, and anger. Remember though, we are all responsible for our own actions. You did not choose for your loved one to have an eating disorder. We (those of us with eating disorders) have made the decision to begin to use food for comfort, whether that is restricting or bingeing. You did not remove the food in our lives or force us to binge and purge. That was our choice and we must take responsibility for it.

Do not feel guilty about not knowing. My parents and Todd both have said at some point, "I feel guilty for not knowing. I should have seen it." I want to say to you: this entire addiction is based on hiding and deception. We become good at it. The feelings of "how did I not know" will haunt you, but those we love are the last ones we want to tell. We cover up from them the most. We don't want to hurt them or fail them and are afraid of being found out. Getting caught up in the feelings of guilt only pleases the enemy and helps no one in the end.

Anger and Hurt: You trusted us. You are bound to be hurt about this. There will be a time to work through that hurt during the recovery process. Anger and resentment only promote more pain. Your first reaction might be to let the person know how deeply they have hurt you, but if you make this solely about *your* hurt and disappointment, it may hinder their ability to trust you and recover.

Love them the way God loves and forgives you. Early on in the recovery, I kept apologizing to Todd. I knew I had hurt him deeply and I felt terrible about it. His response was, "I know you are sorry; let's just get you well." Can you imagine? How could I not work to get better when I had forgiveness like that? Todd has never thrown it back in my face that I had hurt him this way. Instead, he has "wiped my slate clean" just as Christ does for us.

Fear: The fear of what may happen to your loved one is huge. You want to fix it for them, make them well, and take away their pain. This you cannot do. Our addiction is our addiction. Our health can only come from within. It is a walk and journey we must take with God. It is our own personal battle. Know your limitations. You cannot change anyone. However, your prayer, encouragement, and accountability are necessary aspects in that walk and vital in their recovery. Remember God loves them more than you do. Even though your fear is real, put it in perspective and do only what you can to practically help.

Accountability, not Judgment: I wrote about how accountability is an important factor in the recovery process. It stops the cycle of secrecy and lessens the opportunities we have to hide. There is a difference between loving accountability that encourages and judgmental accountability that tears down. Again, it is so important to remember to be an example of how Christ treats you in your sin. Undoubtedly, Todd was frustrated with me and could not understand why I would knowingly jeopardize so much, but he never let me see that. He kept encouraging me to seek Christ every time I failed or resorted back to poor behaviors. Soon, I wasn't afraid of telling him truthfully how I was doing or what I was feeling. I knew there would be no judgment from him, just encouragement and support. Had Todd made it solely about him, instead of just being there for me, I would have continued to hide.

"I just don't understand": "I just don't understand why you do this or how it is helpful. Why can't you just eat like a normal person?" Well, it is an addiction. You aren't going to be able to fully understand unless you are there. You don't have to understand it to be helpful. All you need to know is this is how our pain has manifested itself and we can't just eat like a normal person until we are at a place of spiritual healthiness. Your job is not to understand. Your job is to encourage, love, support them through recovery, and continually direct your loved one back to the eyes of Christ for answers.

How to Talk with a Loved One About Their Disorder

If your child or loved one is showing signs of an eating disorder, you can help. Remember the key is to be a loving example of Christ and to break the cycle of secrecy. Communication is essential.

1. Before approaching your child or loved one, pray about what the Lord wants you to say. Speak through love, not criticism.

2. When you approach your child or loved one, pick a time and place in which you will not be interrupted.

3. Think of specific instances that you felt his or her eating was abnormal. Share with your child or loved one what you have observed that has caused you concern. Express your concerns in a loving, caring manner.

If all is denied and your child or loved one closes the door of communication, try to talk again at a later time. Do not argue about whether there is a problem or not. He or she may not open up at first, but they want to know you care.

Realize that there is a time to talk and a time to listen. Let your child or loved one share with you his or her feelings without placing judgments on them or invalidating how they feel, even if you don't understand and think it is irrational. Ask questions and then listen carefully to the answers. Never take the defensive. If he or she discusses feelings that are hard for you, do not allow yourself to argue. What your child or loved one needs to hear is that you love them and want to help them.

Share truths with them. Tell them they are beautiful, created in God's image, and that He creates masterpieces. Share Scripture that may help and pray with them for strength.

Know When to Act

If your child or loved one embraces your help, give him or her something to go on. Do not leave it at that. Set up an appointment with a doctor or counselor. Never assume that because they tell you that they are doing better or will do better, that it is true. They may tell you what they think you want to hear. People-pleasing and a fear of failure are part of the disorder itself. Watch for healthy signs like eating in a way that is nourishing their body (not abusing it), weight gain (in the case of anorexia), limited trips to the bathroom (in the case of bulimia), a change in overall mind-set, and, most importantly, growth in their walk with Christ and dependency on Him.

If you are concerned that the disorder is already life-threatening or quite serious, do not allow your child or loved one to refuse help. If you are a parent, then you are still the parent, and the child may be in strong denial. Remember, they will only get better when he or she makes that choice, but you may need the help and encouragement of a doctor or counselor before your child or loved one can make that choice on his or her own. If you are a spouse, continue to love and encourage your husband or wife to get help. If you are a friend, support them, but also tell someone in authority in their lives so that further action can be taken to break the cycle of secrecy and find help for them.

Most importantly, *pray, pray, pray* for wisdom for the Lord to show you where to go from here. There is amazing power in prayer, and remember that the answers are always found in Christ.

STEPS FOR PROFESSIONAL HELP

1. A visit to the doctor is imperative. A complete physical is necessary to know how your loved one's physical health has been affected. Listen to the physician for his or her advice on what steps to take next if the eating disorder warrants in-house treatment or hospitalization. He may just refer you to an outpatient counselor or psychiatrist.

2. Choosing an outpatient counselor, psychiatrist, or treatment center is tricky. Most insurance plans do not fully cover this cost, but it may be necessary for the health of your loved one anyway. Do your homework, interview, and ask lots of questions before making a decision. My personal feeling is if there is no spiritual aspect or direction toward Christ, then the recovery will not be life-long. It is merely applying a bandage until the next difficult situation arises.

REFERRAL SITES

www.edreferral.com — referral and information center
www.caringonline.com
www.findingbalance.com
www.Iaedp.com – International Association of Eating Disorder Professionals
www.edap.org -go to treatment referrals
www.nationaleatingdisorders.org – go to treatment referrals or call National Eating Disorder Association 1-800-931-2237

Christian-based Treatment Centers
www.aplaceofhope.com – Whole person care of focusing on the medical, physical, psychological, emotional, nutritional, fitness and spiritual aspects of each person.
www.remudaranch.com east and west campuses
www.rosewoodranch.com
www.selahhouse.net
www.mercyministries.org

Journal Questions

1. How can you be a good influence in your loved one's life and in the way that he or she is eating?

2. What can you tell your loved one about beauty, healthy eating, and exercise that is biblical?

3. What can you do to combat the negative messages from the media?

4. What warning signs do you see in your loved one? Do these warning signs warrant immediate attention from a professional?

5. Do you have feelings of guilt about this disorder in your loved one's life? What can you do about it?

6. How do you feel angry and hurt by your loved one's actions? Can you set your own feelings aside to be able to help your loved one through recovery?

7. How can you keep your fear in check?

8. What steps do you need to take to be a support, to encourage, and to keep your loved one accountable without showing judgment? How can you speak the truth in love?

9. Can you be helpful even if you don't understand? How?

10. How can you break the cycle of secrecy and become a trusted source of support?

11. What are the key elements in the success of talking with your loved one?

Prayer

Dear Heavenly Father,

Help me to be a loving encouragement and support to my loved one as they struggle through this addiction. Help me to keep my eyes on You for my own strength and for wisdom in all of this. Amen.

A Special Message from Leigh-Ann

If you are struggling with a food addiction, my heart goes out to you. If you find comfort in what you are doing, I want you to know that it is a false comfort and it will not last. Please know that you are not alone and that you do not have to remain stuck in these sinking sands for the rest of your life. There is hope in Christ. He is the answer. I encourage you to focus on your worth in Him and find an accountability partner who can also pray for you continually. Your health is dependent on *you*. Only you can change your behaviors. Only you can seek Christ for the answers you need. This is a walk that *you* must take; but you do not have to take it alone. Seek out a counselor or treatment center that will direct you to Christ for answers. Do not wait for tomorrow; tomorrow is already too late. Begin today to find strength in Him and nourish your body the way He intended. If you have a bad day, keep seeking His face. Soon you will see that there will be more days of victory than days of struggle.

Steps to Recovery

The key to success and freedom from eating disorders is to realize that the physical, emotional, and spiritual realms all must work toward growth simultaneously. I cannot give you a one, two, three-step guideline to wellness. In fact, I have failed at recovery many times trying to follow them, but what I can tell you is if there isn't growth in Christ, then recovery is only temporary. It is impossible to work through the emotional pain without the spiritual in place. Likewise, it is impossible to manage the physical without the spiritual. However, the very nature of eating disorders can be critical and life-threatening. You may not be able to wait until you have it right with God to begin to eat in a way that is vital for your life. You may have to begin this process with help and support until you can do it on your own. This is why I say that all aspects must work together simultaneously for optimal recovery. Baby steps of right choices in each area lead to significant, lasting growth. Recovery should look like a slow, steady incline instead of rapid rise and falls. What your recovery looks like is evidence of where your heart is.

Emotional
- Discover what is at the root of your hurt and pain, desire for control, or fear of failure.
  - If necessary, seek counseling for this.
  - Take it to God.
  - Move into forgiveness.

Spiritual
- Examine your heart—choose whom you are going to listen to.
- Recognize the eating disorder as sin—choose to become a person of integrity.
- Sit at God's feet in confession and in prayer; listen to His voice and follow as He leads.
- Study God's Word to discover who He is, His character, and His truth.
- Hide God's Word in your heart to combat the lies from the enemy.
- Apply biblical truths to your life. Accept that you are His child, His masterpiece, and His reflection, created to reflect His character.
- Choose to trust, follow, and obey.

Physical
- Relinquish control factors (Chapter 11).
- Choose to eat to nourish your body and within God's will (Chapter 13).
- Check out helpful hints in Chapter 13.

I am praying for strength for all who seek His face. You can do it with Him!

Blessings,
Leigh-Ann

Works Cited

Chapter 1
1.www.anred.com/stats.html
www.state.sc.us/dmh/anorexia/statistics.htm

Chapter 2
1. www.mirror-mirror.org/anorexia-statistics.htm

Chapter 3
1.www.eatingdisorderinfo.org/5.html
2.www.eatingdisorderinfo.org/18.html
www.eatingdisorderinfo.org/6.html

Chapter 4
1. www.anred.com/causes.html

Chapter 5
1.www.healthyplace.com/Communities/Eating_Disorders/
consequences_4.asp
2.www.eatingdisorderinfo.org/5.html
3.www.eatingdisorderinfo.org/18.html
4.www.anred.com
5.www.eatingdisorder.org/about_the_center/research.php
6.Marcia Germaine Hutchinson, *Transforming Body Image;
Love the Body You Have* (Freedom, California: The Crossing
Press, 1985)137

Chapter 7
1.www.anred.com/stats.html

Chapter 9
1. David Parkes, *My Father's Chair*, Irish Records, 1998.

Chapter 10
1.Shannon Ethridge and Stephen Arterburn, *Every Young Woman's Battle,* Waterbrook Press, 2004.

Chapter 11
1.Shannon Ethridge and Stephen Arterburn, *Every Young Woman's Battle*, Waterbrook Press, 2004.

Chapter 12
1. Julianna Slattery, *Beyond the Masquerade*, Tyndale House Publishers, 2007.
2. Sinclair Ferguson, *A Heart for God*, Banner of Truth, 1987)

Chapter 13
1. Stormie Omartian, *Just Enough Light for the Step I'm On*, Harvest House Publishers, 1999.
2. Bill Phillips, *Body for Life*, Collins, 1999.

Chapter 14
1.www.tentmaker.org/quotes

Chapter 15
1.Philip Yancey, *Where Is God When It Hurts?*, Zondervan, 1990.
2.Author Unknown
3. Stormie Omartian, *Just Enough Light for the Step I'm On*, Harvest House Publishers, 1999.

Chapter 16
1.Christina Aguilera, *Reflection*, RCA, 1999.